MEMORIES
of a
DEPRESSION BABY

How a family of ten survived the depression

Kayene,
Thank you, you are such a
treat and brighten my day.
Is am healing quickly.
My best always
Margie

MEMORIES
of a
DEPRESSION BABY

How a family of ten survived the depression

By
BILL WILLIAMS

LEATHERS
PUBLISHING

A division of Squire Publishers, Inc.
4500 College Blvd.
Leawood, KS 66211
1/888/888-7696

Copyright 2001
Printed in the United States

ISBN: 1-58597-086-7

A division of Squire Publishers, Inc.
4500 College Blvd.
Leawood, KS 66211
1/888/888-7696

Acknowledgements

I would like to dedicate this book to my wonderful wife, Margie, of 45 years, without whom I could never have started this book, and to my son, Bob, and his wife, Cindy, who gave encouragement, and to our grandchildren, Tim, Karie and Melissa, who will carry on the tradition of values which saw a family of ten through the depression and two wars.

I would also like to dedicate this book to my parents and to my brothers and sisters, Bud, France, Jim, John, Sis, Titter and Babe. There will never be another family like it. TOO BAD!!!

Preface

I write here the memorable events of my life, not in a boastful way, because many people of my time had similar experiences and surpassed mine many times over. I cannot write about the experiences of others, but only mine.

I put my memories to paper, not because my life is so unique, but to preserve bits and pieces of a family, growing and living in a time when America was younger and more naive. When seeing an airplane fly overhead was an exciting event; when listening to a radio and hearing a voice come through a box from miles away seemed impossible. A time when a telephone was not available to a large number of people, unless you happened to know a neighbor who was a little better off than you; when going barefoot during the summer months was a necessity, not an option.

I wish not to glorify my experiences, but to give credit to the couple who saw a family of eight children through one of the most difficult periods of the Twentieth Century, my Mom and Pop! My seven brothers and sisters and I owe so much to parents who gave all they had to keep us fed, clothed and sheltered during a time when surviving was a day-to-day thing. Our parents saw that we all had an opportunity to go to school and graduate from high school. College was not an option for most of us, but what we lacked in a formal higher education was made up by life experiences, and all eight of us turned out to be upstanding, law-abiding, hard-working, self-sufficient adults with families of our own.

Mom and Pop are deceased now, along with five of my brothers and sisters, Bud, Jim, France, John and Sis. My reason for writing my memoirs is to pass on to all the children of my family and to all their children what special people their grandparents were. They died without fanfare. They were born, they lived and they died. But there is so much more to tell between their birthdates and the date they died. I will do my best to fill in this large gap.

Prologue

Tuesday, October 29, 1929 —"Black Tuesday" the stock market crashed!

Never again would the people of America be as confident. Soup lines would become a way of life. Nearly 30 per cent of Americans would be out of work. Young men who could not find work would leave home seeking a way to survive. Whole families would pick up and move, carrying with them all their possessions, and travel half way across America seeking work. Many did not survive the ordeal.

But, the work ethics instilled in many of the families allowed them to survive "The Great Depression." My parents were of that group.

Table of Contents

CHAPTER 1

Our Family Beginnings

MY DAD, Franklin Floyd Williams, "Pop," as we all called him, and I shall, from now on, was born April 25, 1889, in Rogers, Arkansas, to Preston LaFayette and Lucinda Estella (Roll) Williams. Preston was married previously and had a son by that union, Paris E. I have found little information on this marriage, but did know my step-uncle, Paris, and his wife, Martha. Pop had two older sisters, Annetta and Mildred, and an older brother, Charles.

Pop's family moved from Rogers, Arkansas, to Elk River, Missouri, in McDonald County and were living there at the time of the 1900 census. It was at that time that Pop was befriended by an Indian chief who taught him some of the Cherokee language. Pop would speak some of the language and count to 10 when we would press him as children. Elk River is located in the southwestern corner of Missouri and adjacent to the Arkansas and Oklahoma state lines.

From Elk River, the family moved to northern Missouri and settled in Buchanan County and the area of the city of St. Joseph.

The 1910 census shows the children living with their mother and Pop's older brother, Charles, as head of the house-

Uncle Charlie and Pop
Circa 1909

hold. Preston dropped from the scene. I have no more information on Preston, but the family was living on a farm with the head of the family, Charles, and with Pop listed as a farmhand.

Mom's family consisted of her father, Jacob Samuel Blakley; mother, Sarah Magdalene; two sisters, Vernie and Minnie; and one brother, Roy. Jacob's grandparents had immigrated from England and settled in the St. Joseph, Missouri area.

Mom's mother died in 1902. Mom was eight years old at the time. Grandpa Jacob tried to care for the family, but could not, and he gave the children to other families to raise. Mom and sisters, Vernie and Minnie, were taken in by the Dougherty family, parents of Sarah Magdalene, Mom's mother. Their brother, Roy, went to another family. Grandpa took off and the children would not hear from him for many years.

Mom was raised by the Dougherty family, a farming family. She grew up cooking, washing, cleaning and all the other chores associated with farming; almost a slave, but was treated well and probably worked no harder than if she had been their own daughter. All women worked sunup to sundown, cooking huge meals for the family and even larger meals during harvest season. Mom was the best cook and I'd put her up against anyone! I never saw her use a recipe or a measuring spoon. She could turn out a large super meal in no time. This would come in handy in feeding her own large

2

family, and her experience in the kitchen would be invaluable during the depression when she was forced to feed all of us with practically no money for food. I understand why Pop fell in love and married Mom!! She had a great sense of humor, which never left her even in the worst of times, and I guess that trait carried over to all her children.

Pop only went to the eighth grade. He was needed on the farm. A number of boys and girls finished their schooling by the eighth grade. America, for the most part, was a farming society and the youth were needed to do the work, which was mostly manual. The eight years of education they received was far superior to the first eight years of education a child receives today. The three "R's" were stressed and little time was left in the day for sports or play.

I never once saw Pop use a pad and pencil to figure a math problem. It was all done in his head. You could almost hear the wheels turning when he was figuring a problem pertaining to land acreage or the number of rods in a fence line, the number of posts or rolls of barbed wire needed to fence in a field or pasture. The things he learned in school were used every day on the farm.

Pop taught Sunday school when he was a young man and after he was married. He was forced to give it up when the family and work took all his time. Pop could recite all the Books of the Bible from memory and would do so when we pressed him.

Pop married Beulah Elizabeth Blakley on December 24, 1913, Christmas Eve. Pop was 24 and Mom, 19 years of age.

3

Pop with two of his horses, Circa 1913

Pop had become quite a farmer and had his own farm when he married Mom, and was doing quite well. Pop was quite debonair as a young man. Mom would tell of his dress and also his appreciation of fine horses.

* * * * * * * * *

Mom and Pop's first child was a son, Floyd (Pop's middle name) Charles, born in 1914. He died at the age of two. The newspaper clipping I have seen listed his death as a victim of "summer complaint." Mom told me in later years that "summer complaint" was a commonly used term for a flu-like condition that took many lives. I could tell how much Floyd's death hurt Mom and Pop when she would talk about him. A death which could probably have been prevented today with antibiotics. I know very little about my brother, Floyd, as he lived such a short time, but I do remember seeing pictures of him. The whereabouts of said pictures are unknown today, probably lost to all in one of the many moves the family made throughout the years.

In the same year of Floyd's death, 1916, Mom gave birth on November 4th to a second son, Franklin Leroy. I believe Frank's birth helped in a small way to relieve the hurt in losing Floyd.

Frank, nicknamed "Bud," was born in DeKalb, Missouri. In the future I will refer to Frank as Bud. Pop was farming and doing very well. He always prided himself in having some of the finest horses around and in being an all-around good farmer.

On April 28, 1918, a son, Francis Walter, was born. We called him "France." When France was about a year or so, Pop bought his first automobile. It was a "Pilot," a touring car with a canvas top. Mom never learned to drive an automobile, but did drive a horse and buggy. She would load Bud and France and drive to visit neighbors and run errands, as Pop was kept busy on the farm.

Mom tells that on one occasion while returning home from visiting a neighbor, "it came up a storm." The buggy she was driving had a top, so she continued home in the storm. The roads were narrow and dirt, which soon turned

The Pilot, Mom and Pop's first car. Mom in rear holding France, Bud in front. Circa 1919.

5

to mud. She was urging the horse on in the downpour and dim late evening light when the horse suddenly snorted and rared up, letting out a loud whinny. Mom tugged at the reins to settle the horse down. In the fading light, she saw the body of an old woman laying beside the road. Mom had seen the old woman before walking the roads. It was speculated that she had been hit by lightning. When Mom would recount this story, you could see the fear still showing in her eyes, even after these many years. I guess this story made a deep impression on me when hearing it at an early age, as I never forgot it!

Mom also told us a story that I believed to be true at the time, because Mom would not lie to her children. It seems that in the mid-1800s a young couple living in a small rural community got married on a hot summer day at the farm home of the bride. Shortly after the wedding vows had been exchanged, the new bride collapsed and died. It was suspected heat stroke. In those days, a body did not keep long in the hot summer heat, so it was decided to bury her that afternoon. A grave was dug in the family cemetery, and the new bride was buried in her wedding attire. A man who had attended the wedding and the funeral thought it a shame that the huge diamond wedding ring, which the bride was wearing when she was buried, should remain buried. He went to the grave that night and dug up the coffin and tried to get the wedding ring off the swollen finger of the bride, but was unsuccessful. He pulled his pocket knife out and cut off the finger of the bride to get the ring. The blood began to flow, and the bride fluttered her eyelids and sat up in the coffin. The grave robber was terrified and ran for his life. The bride climbed from the grave and walked to her farm home. It was said that the bride had only been unconscious when buried, and the blood flowing from the amputated finger had stimulated her heart and had revived her. Mom would tell this story at night and, in the glow of the lamp light, it would make this story more frightening. I still don't know if this story was true, but Mom didn't lie to her children.

Life was good to Pop, Mom, Bud and France at this time. Prices were good for farm products and they were living well. They owned their farm, had bought their first automobile and were looking to increase the size of the farm by buying more land. The 1st World War was in progress, and it looked like prices would remain good for farm products. (Pop, being a farmer, was deferred from serving at this time.) Pop mortgaged the farm and bought more land and everything looked good. Then the war ended and shortly afterwards prices began to fall. It wasn't long before farm prices dropped through the floor. Pop not only lost the new farm land, but lost the home farm to the bank. Pop told me a story about how bad the prices for hogs were at that time. He said a farmer shipped a carload of hogs by rail to the Chicago market where prices were higher. When he received his freight bill from the railroad, it was more than he had received for the sale of the hogs.

* * * * * * * * * *

Pop had always liked his home in Arkansas, and I think he and Mom and family took a trip to Rogers to see if things were any better. As it turned out, they were not, and Mom was homesick, so they headed back to Missouri. At least, they had relatives and family in DeKalb. It was December 1920 when they were driving through Bolivar, Missouri, and Mom was "with child." It was there in Bolivar, Missouri, that my sister decided to be born. She was named Beulah (after Mom) Fern. Can you think of a more inopportune time to be born? After a few days, they proceeded back to DeKalb, Missouri, with the new addition to the family.

7

Prospects for a better livelihood were still bleak in northern Missouri, so Pop and Mom decided to move to Pueblo, Colorado, as Pop had heard of jobs with the railroad in that area. Pop was able to land a job with the Denver Rio Grande Railroad as an inspector. His job as brake inspector was one he really enjoyed. I often heard him say in later years that he would liked to have made railroading a career. The freight trains would come down out of the mountains around Denver, and the brakes would have to be applied to keep the train speed down. In Pueblo, the brakes, wheels, axle bearing boxes, called "hot boxes," would have to be inspected. In the process of the train braking, the wheels would become heated and hot. In some cases, the overheated wheels would ignite the packing around the axle. The resulting fire could possibly cause the bearing to seize, locking up the wheel, causing wear on one spot of the wheel and possibly causing the car to jump the tracks, resulting in a derailment. The inspection job was crucial to the safe operation of the train. I'm sure Pop was a good inspector and dedicated to his job.

Mom gave birth to another son on October 31, 1922, James **Blakley**, Mom's maiden name. Mom and Pop were going to name all the children using the letter "F"; Floyd, Frank, Francis and Fern, but ran out of names with the letter "F." Mom had a lot of problems with the altitude in Pueblo and had difficulty breathing. Her problem continued to get worse, so Pop finally had to quit his job and the family moved back to Missouri. I'm sure Pop hated to give up his railroad job, but Mom's health was more important. I still have Pop's railroad watch, which Mom gave me shortly after Pop died. It's a large pocket watch with a steam locomotive embossed on the lid of the watch, which pops open, revealing the face of the watch. I'll pass it on to our son some day.

* * * * * * * * * *

Work around DeKalb was still hard to find, but Pop was a hard worker and they were able to survive by working for other farmers in the area. He worked for Walter Head, who was Director of the Boy Scouts of America. About 1926, Pop heard that Kansas City, Missouri was in the process of building some new buildings, City Hall and other large high-rise type buildings.

The family once again pulled up stakes and made a move, this time to Kansas City, Missouri. Pop was able to get a job with a construction company, building some of the high-rise buildings. Pop was never afraid of heights, so he hired on as a high steel worker. The family rented a house in Kansas City, and on June 12, 1927, Mom gave birth to their sixth child, a daughter, Helen Marie, who would later be nicknamed "Titter."

On Tuesday, October 29, 1929, which became known as "Black Tuesday," the stock market crashed and overnight things changed. Pop and Mom had no investments in the stock market, but they were to feel the effects for the next several years, as well as almost every other American.

The family then moved to a farm in Clay County, Missouri, which was in North Kansas City. The job Pop had with the construction company was about to come to an end. But before that happened, Mom gave birth to their seventh child, a son, William Robert, May 23, 1930. That son was **me**, and I believe I was named for my uncle, **William** Sherman Crowe. Mom said I cried for the next two years, which was probably because I was hungry, and getting enough to eat was going to be a problem for several years.

When I was born in 1930, the President was Herbert Hoover; Vice President, Charles Curtis. Life expectancy was 59.7 years, and the Dow Jones Average was 137. The average income was $1,937. A new car could be bought for $610; a loaf of bread was $.09, and a gallon of gas was $.10. Milk

9

was selling for $.56 a gallon, and gold was $20.67 per ounce, and with the depression, things would get worse.

* * * * * * * * * * *

With the depression now in full swing, the building boom in Kansas City ended, and Pop and Mom again packed up and moved the family to Beverly, Missouri. It was a small town north and east of Kansas City and just north of Leavenworth, Kansas, situated on the east bank of the Missouri River. The reason for all the directions is because it's hard to locate on the map. Pop rented a farm which was right on the bank of the Missouri River, the "Big Muddy," as it was known. It was really a desolate place to live. It was hot in the summer and cold in the winter. Summer saw the river marshes become a breeding ground for millions of mosquitoes and other insects, not to mention snakes. Winter snow and ice made it almost impossible to go anywhere. It was known as the *Island*. With snow thaws in spring and fall rains, it was surrounded by water. And in this desolate place on December 5, 1931, number eight child was born, John Leo. John once said of the place where he was born, **"It wasn't the end of the world**, but you could sure see it from our back porch."

The Federal Prison in Leavenworth, Kansas, which was just across the Missouri River from Beverly, had a prison farm on the Missouri side of the river. The inmates of the prison farm were all minimum security and worked the farm. The farm consisted of a large dairy, hog and beef operation and chickens, along with field crops. The inmates would be working near our home on occasions, and sometimes they would give us a candy bar or some other treat. I guess we must have been in poverty because the inmates took pity on us. Pop was doing some farming as well as working wherever he could make a dollar or two.

Bud, France and Beulah (nicknamed "Sis," so I will refer to her as Sis from now on) attended the high school in Weston, Missouri, which was a small town north of Beverly approximately ten miles. Weston was also on the Missouri River, but was on higher ground. Weston was a nice, small town.

Things in Beverly weren't all bad. The people were friendly and would get together every July 4th for a large *ice cream social*. I was just becoming old enough to remember some outstanding events, like the candy bar, "Mister Good Bar," given us by the prison farm inmates, the ice cream social in the summer, driving to Weston to see the free movies on Saturday evening, which were shown on a large screen outdoors on the town square, or the time Mom hosted the Beverly Better Homes Club, of which she was a member. Mom served coffee and a cake she had baked. She used her nice small green glass dessert plates that she kept hidden and would bring out for special occasions. It happened that one of the little green plates also served as a soap dish by the kitchen sink, when they weren't being used on special occasions. Mom would always wash it and use it as she did the day the Beverly Better Homes Club met. I guess Mom must have dropped through the floor when I told one of the ladies that she was eating from the soap dish. I don't recall Mom ever hosting the Beverly Better Homes Club after that day.

I remember one night coming home from one of the free movies in Weston, Pop was driving an old truck with Mom in front holding John, the youngest, and the rest of us were all riding in the back of the truck. All were standing, holding on to the sideboards, except me. I was sitting on the floor. I suddenly spotted a fifty-cent piece on the floor of the truck. I clutched it in my hot little hand until we arrived home, where I told everyone.

11

Not knowing who had lost it, in the back of the truck were several friends of Bud and France, Mom decided we should all share in the good fortune. The next day, being Sunday, Mom suggested we buy the ingredients and make ice cream in our old 1-1/2 gallon, crank-type ice cream freezer. We bought ice, salt and whatever Mom needed to make the ice cream. While Mom was fixing Sunday dinner, Pop and the rest of us took turns turning the crank on the ice cream freezer. The smallest members would start turning; it was much easier in the beginning, but it took real muscle power the harder the ice cream became, so Bud and France would finish it.

When the ice cream was ready, it would be covered with an old towel, so it would further harden

We would all go in and eat Sunday dinner. After dinner, we all grabbed a bowl and Bud served up the ice cream. Bud always took the paddle as it seemed to contain a very large portion, but he was the oldest!

* * * * * * * * * *

I was too young to remember when the following incident occurred, but I remember hearing about it while sitting around the kitchen table. (A little side note, our kitchen table, a large table with room enough for the whole family to sit during meals, was a forum for all to talk. The old adage, "Children should be seen and not heard," was part of our upbringing, and since we usually had nothing to add to the conversation, we became good listeners.) On with the incident ... on our rental farm in Beverly, Missouri, was a pasture where we kept our milk cow. Being in close proximity to the "big muddy," the pasture would become inundated with river water. Being a marshy pasture, a large number of saplings would sprout up when the weather turned warm.

There was always plenty of seed to blow over the pasture; the river banks were lined with trees. It was Jim's job during the summer to take a wide blade knife, called a "corn knife," and cut the little saplings down before they grew to such a size as to shade out the pasture. In using a corn knife, you swung down at a 45-degree angle as close to the ground as possible. The resulting cut would leave a small stump with a sharp point sticking up. Jim's other chore was to milk "old bossy" morning and night. Bud and France were exempt from these chores because from sunup till sundown they had jobs working in the fields for farmers making a dollar a day and saving most of it to help pay for their education.

One evening, the flies were extremely numerous when Jim was milking "old bossy," and bossy was frantically trying to keep the pesky flies off her back by using her only weapon, her tail. Each time she would swing her tail, Jim's head would receive the full blow. As this battle between old bossy's tail and Jim's head grew at a fever pitch, something had to give. It was the end of old bossy's tail. Jim had grabbed the corn knife and, as if cutting a sapling, whacked off the bushy end of old bossy's tail. As old bossy frantically tried to fight off the flies with the stump of a tail, spraying a tiny stream of blood all about the barn, as well as on Jim and the half pail of milk that old bossy had already surrendered, Pop arrived home about this time and found Jim and old bossy in battle. Pop sided with old bossy and grabbed one of the saplings that Jim had cut that day and came at Jim. One thing I learned about my brother Jim, he wasn't stupid! He had the good sense to run. He took off across the pasture with Pop in full pursuit. Pop was fast, but Jim was running for his life and might have made the river, but for the stump of a sapling. Jim tripped and fell, his chin coming down on the sharp edge of another sapling stump, splitting his chin open. This ended the chase, and Pop, the aggressor, suddenly

13

became the rescuer. The scar the sapling stump left gave Jim a Kirk Douglas look. Old bossy came through the battle with probably a better weapon than before. Instead of swishing flies off, she could now club them to death.

I think it was in the spring of 1934 or 1935 that the "big muddy" flooded and Pop could see that the crops would be very meager that year, so we packed up and moved to Weston, Missouri, some ten miles away. I guess the thinking was that since the older children were going to high school in Weston, it would make sense to move closer to that city.

It was about this time I began remembering more events. I do not remember the move to Weston, but I recall some of the events that took place while we lived there. We lived at 400 Ashley at the bottom of a steep hill. A house at the top of the hill had some apple trees. John and I went up the hill one day and climbed the fence and grabbed a couple of apples. A man came out of the house and chased us down the hill. We had dropped the apples and ended up with nothing except a good lesson about what happens when you covet a neighbor's apples.

Brother Jim was about 12 years old, and I remember an old bike with no handlebars that he was working on. Jim took the tongue from an old coaster wagon and fastened it to the bike where the handlebar would have been. I can still see him flying down the hill, steering the bike with that old wagon tongue.

Directly behind our house was a large barn that faced the street behind us. It was kept full of cars. I don't know who owned it. One day it caught on fire, and I remember the neighbors helping to get the old cars out of the barn. It was an exciting day! The Weston Volunteer Fire Department arrived and, after a busy day, finally put the fire out. This was all very exciting to a small five-year-old boy.

Bud, France and Sis were going to Weston High, whose

school colors were blue and white. I can still see Bud and France wearing their letter sweaters; they played football. Bud was one year ahead of France and had a somewhat larger build. Bud played on the line as tackle and France would play in the backfield. Working in the fields, cutting and sawing wood would build the strength needed to play football. Weight lifting was seen as a waste of valuable work time and energy.

Bud graduated from Weston High in 1934 and France in 1935. Sis would not graduate from Weston as she was a couple of years younger than France, and we were again going to move. This time to Kansas and to the small farming community of Kickapoo, a *very small* town in Kickapoo township, with only one small store, a couple of churches and a combined feed store and gas station. Kickapoo was almost due west of Weston and on the west side of the Missouri River. Most people around Kickapoo would drive the ten miles to Leavenworth to do their shopping. You probably won't find Kickapoo on any map today because the town itself no longer exists. When we moved to Kickapoo, there were two one-room grade schools, with eight grades in each school. High school students, 9 through 12, had to get themselves to one of two high schools, one Catholic and one public, in Leavenworth. The two grade schools in the Kickapoo area were about four miles apart; one being in the small town of Kickapoo itself and the other one, Coffin school, about four miles closer to Leavenworth. When we moved from Weston to Kickapoo, we were about one mile from the Coffin school and three miles from the Kickapoo grade school.

CHAPTER 2

Our Stay in Kickapoo

THE FAMILY MOVED into a large farm house which was rented from the Baskas family. There were several acres of farming land and a large wooded area which ran along Plum Creek. The road that ran along the front of the property dropped off and ran down a fairly steep hill to a bridge which crossed over Plum Creek. The proof of a powerful car that you could take pride in was to make it up Plum Creek hill in high gear. You could see the cars about a mile before they reached the hill, speeding up to a high speed, hoping to achieve the ultimate goal, no down-shifting. In rainy weather, the dirt road would be muddy, and it became even more difficult to top the hill in high gear. The old cars and trucks would fish-tail in the mud and sometimes end up in the ditch.

Pop was no different than all the other drivers, and since we lived or farmed in the area for several years, John and I, when riding with Pop, would come to know that hill first-hand. Pop, John and I would experience the AGONY OF DEFEAT when, on more than one occasion, the old car would almost get to the top only to start slowing to a crawl, and Pop would have to down shift to second gear. But Pop was not about to be defeated by some stupid hill. The old car we were riding in would slow to a snail's pace and the engine would arrive at that critical stall speed. Pop would begin a rocking motion trying to help that old car over the crest. Sometimes it would help and we would creep over the summit, and we could see a slight smile on Pop's lips as though he had triumphed Mt. Everest. There is a new blacktop road now, and the old Plum Creek hill has been somewhat leveled off. The younger generation that travels that road today don't give that hill a thought as they drive their powerful modern cars and trucks. It's just a small bump in the road.

****

The Baskas farm that we rented was a large two-story stucco home which was a blessing for a large family. The Weston home had been a lot smaller, three bedrooms. We now had four bedrooms. Mom and Pop always had their own room, except when one of us was a baby, then we shared the room with them. In a three-bedroom house, the boys shared one room and the girls the other. The boys were more crowded; there were more of us. The girls' room was about to become less spacious. Number nine, a girl, Juanita Louise, was born on October 27, 1936. Mom and Pop never talked about sex or anything to do with reproduction, so when we, the younger ones, asked where our baby sister came from, Pop would say she had been found in the cabbage patch, or the stork left her. I guess we had no reason to question Pop, it sounded natural to us, although I never found a baby in the cabbage patch. Pop picked the name, Juanita, from a song by the same name. He liked the name, Juanita did not. When she was older, she chose to go by her middle name, Louise.

On the Baskas farm were several ponies and small riding horses that belonged to the owner. We did a lot of riding that summer. I was six the summer of 1936 and was old enough to ride one of the smaller ponies. Jim was quite a good rider and learned the trick of mounting over the rear end of the horse by running up behind the horse, placing his hands on the rump and hopping into the saddle. He had seen this in one of the few western movies; probably *Tom Mix*.

Bud and France worked on other farms during the summer. Usually, the work was for small wages, but included room and board. Pop also would work for other farmers in the area, plowing, planting, cultivating and harvesting. Sometimes he would drive trucks for them hauling grain to the elevator, hauling feed and helping during the haying season.

We had some farm land on the rented farm and some of the free time that Pop, Bud and France had was spent putting in some crops for themselves. I recall Bud and France using the old iron-wheel John Deere tractor which came with the farm, plowing and planting. You could always tell a John Deere tractor. The pop-pop-popping the engine made was very distinctive and could be heard for miles on a clear summer morning.

Bud and France had earned enough to purchase an automobile. Bud purchased an Auburn, a huge touring car, green in color with a white canvas top and whitewall tires. It was the prettiest car I had ever seen. It is less remembered than the Cord, which was built by the Auburn/Cord Automobile Co. France bought a smaller car, a Nash, I think, which also had a canvas top. On this farm were several goats which we, as a family, didn't particularly care for, but they belonged to the owner of the farm and we had no choice but to care for them. One morning as I was just getting out of bed, I heard a commotion from the back yard. I peered out of the window and saw France chasing a goat. The goat was leading France all over the yard and finally jumped a fence and escaped. France went over to his car and was showing Mom what the goat had done to the canvas top of his car.

The goat had apparently been on the canvas roof of the car, and the sharp little hoofs had punched several holes in the canvas top. France was fuming; the goats that day did nothing to endear themselves to France.

There was a large barn behind the house; John and I would play in the barn. We would climb the wooden ladder to the loft and play in the hay. It sure made a neat playhouse. One day we were in the loft and decided to jump from the loft to a pile of hay down below. John jumped first and landed in the hay on his little bottom — no problem. Now, it was my turn. I slid off the edge of the loft and lit on my feet. Unknown to us, there was a board with a large nail in it sticking straight up. I hit that nail with the heel of my right foot and drove that nail into my heel (we were barefooted.) about two inches. I couldn't pull it out, so I ran to the house screaming with that board dragging along firmly attached to my heel. I remember not being able to sleep, and Mom would have me soaking my foot in warm salt water for hours at a time.

I guess it healed okay, because in September I started my schooling as a first grader at the Coffin school. Being a shy person, I would hide behind Mom's apron whenever company would come to the door. I on one side, and John on the other, peering out as if hiding from some unknown danger. Starting to school was a very traumatic experience for me. I really didn't know what to expect. You would think that with a large number of brothers and sisters that I would be prepared. But my brothers and sisters were so much older that I never had been involved in their activities, and none of them ever had the time to work with me. Mom was busy from sunup to sundown cooking, washing and all the thousands of other things that were necessary to care for a large family. Pop worked the same hours as Mom, trying to keep us clothed, fed and warm in the winter. Bud and France were

Left: Titter
3rd Grade
Coffin School, 1936

Right: Bill
1st Grade
Coffin School,
Kickapoo, 1936

seldom home as they were working, either with Pop cutting wood to sell or working for other farmers. I think what little I really knew about school would come from Helen, who would be affectionately called "Titter." (When Helen was born, Jim, who was only four or five years old, had trouble with the word, "sister", and it came out as "titter"; Helen would forever become "Titter" to the family.") Titter was three years older than I and in the third grade when I started as a first grader at Coffin school.

Coffin school was a one-room school with a big "pot-belly" stove toward the rear of the room. I think it was toward the rear as I don't remember ever turning around to look to the rear, because the first day of school, Miss Muffin, the teacher, laid down the rules and not turning around must have been one of them, along with the other usual "do's and don'ts." No talking unless called upon, raising your hand and getting acknowledged before asking a question, raising one finger to go to the bathroom, which was one of two small outhouses outside and to the side of the school building; raising two fingers if we were to have a bowel movement. Very complicated instructions for a backward first grader. Not long after being given these bathroom signals, I had forgotten which was which. Not remembering which was which proved a disaster for the little first grade girl who sat directly behind me. One morning just before recess, it became apparent to me that I was not going to be able to control my bladder till recess, but what were those signals? I tried to remember which was which — one finger or two. I was probably thinking that I should have paid more attention when Miss Muffin gave us the rules. Anyway, while all this was going through my head, my bladder gave up the battle and my urine was going down my pant leg. I probably thought no one will know the difference because I did keep a straight face. I think I might have gotten away with it but for the girl sitting behind. When the water began soaking her feet, she let out a yell and jumped out of her seat. The yelling violated all the rules. Miss Muffin realized at that time that she had a real challenge on her hands. My punishment — to spend the rest of the day in wet overalls and standing all alone on the school yard during recess.

Jim, being one of two eighth graders, had the job of putting up the American flag every morning and helping, along with his classmate, to start the fire in the pot-belly stove on cold fall mornings. I was so proud of Jim, my big brother, given all the responsibility.

There were less than twenty students in the entire eight grades. Each class sat together in its own little group. The first thing in the morning we would recite the Pledge of Allegiance. The teacher would then go to each group in the morning, after giving out the general news of the day, and give them their assignment for the next hour. She usually started with the eighth grade and would go down through all the grades. She would spend time with each student as needed. As I think back, I can't remember one thing I learned at Coffin school except my hand signals.

Going from a home where a child was "seen and not heard," a home which we seldom left, never playing with children, except for brothers and sisters, our own age. There was no radio, television, newspaper or books for a small child.

I was completely in the dark as to what my role was as a first grader. I never knew enough to ask questions. It was really a scary situation for a six-year-old to be in. I could write my first name, Billy, but had no idea how to spell my last name. A large family has a language all its own, and it was very different from anything I heard at Coffin school.

We had several horses and ponies on the farm we had rented from the Baskas family, as previously mentioned. Jim would ride a horse to school, along with several other children. There was a small stable with hitching rail and watering tank not far from the school building itself; the horses were kept tied up there during the day. Each rider would bring his own hay and grain for his horse. The rest of us either walked the mile or so to school or would get a ride from a family member. We usually walked, Titter and I, as Pop would leave for work at daylight. Once in a while Bud or France would give us a ride if it fit into their schedule. We would walk with other kids; as we passed their farms, they would join the group and there would be several of us arriving at school at the same time.

****

One morning Pop and Mom were going to Leavenworth to shop for food (Pop must have gotten paid for his work) and to buy me a pair of bib overalls, Big Mac. Whenever they bought me overalls, which wasn't very often, they would get the largest size that I could wear. It probably wasn't because I needed new overalls, but more than likely John had nothing to wear. So the overalls I was wearing, which were just beginning to fit, went to John, and I again had to break in another oversized bib overalls. The five of us drove to town, Mom, Pop, John, Babe and I. Jim and Titter went to school. After buying the "big" new bib overalls, I changed in the car on the way back to school. The "big" new "Big Mac" overalls had to be rolled up with three big cuffs and the suspenders had to be taken up as far as they would go, resulting in the bib ending up right under my chin. Mom and Pop knew it would be a long time before I would need another new pair of "Big Mac" overalls. John was envious of me getting a new pair, and I was mad at John for getting my overalls, which finally began to fit. I never owned a pair that fit; John didn't either, mine were too big for him!

We took our lunch to school every day, but that morning Mom had nothing in the house for lunches, so Jim and Titter had not taken a lunch to school that morning. Mom had promised that I would bring their lunches when they dropped me off from our trip to town. We arrived at the Coffin school just before lunchtime and Pop dropped me off. You've got to picture this scene: a six-year-old, about to enter a classroom full of students at work, wearing a pair of new "Big Mac" overalls three sizes too big with cuffs four inches wide and the bib at chin level; three lunch bags in his arms with bananas sticking from the top of each bag. When I ran into that classroom with the huge pant legs swishing together and yelling at the top of my voice, "We've got bananas for lunch," Jim and Titter must have dropped through the floor. Bananas were something we seldom had at home.

Sis was attending high school in Leavenworth, and it was quite a chore for her to get to school. She would ride with families who also had children in high school. Sometimes Bud or France would drive her to school.

Our life in the big home with all the extras came to an end at the end of the year 1936. Our lease was up, or whatever agreement we had with the owner, and we once again moved. This time it was to a small house just outside the town of Kickapoo and near the one-room school of Kickapoo. Once again, a steep hill came in to play. The little town of

24

Kickapoo was on fairly level ground, but the terrain dropped off toward the Missouri River. A steep hill with a dirt road led down to where our house sat at the end of the road. There was only one way out, up the steep dirt road with the little town sitting at the top. The one-room school sat at the top of the hill and looked down directly on our house.

I began attending Kickapoo school after the Christmas break, along with Jim and Titter. It was a shorter route to school by climbing the steep hill rather than going by the road. The road circled the steep hill and led away from the school, so we climbed the hill every day. (Mrs. Sharpe was our teacher.)

We moved into our (rented) small house (small for a family of 10), just before Christmas 1936. I remember we were there for Christmas because the gift I received from Mom and Pop was a small bow-and-arrow set, the one with the little rubber suction cups on the end of the arrows. I hadn't had the little bow and arrow set for more than an hour when I shot John in the forehead with the little suction arrow, which stuck. Mom hid the little bow-and-arrow set for a few days. John received a little celluloid reindeer. I recall Jim going out and cutting the cedar Christmas tree and dragging it home. It was good to have the whole family together for the holiday. We always had a good time.

Pop had raised some popcorn during the summer so we would always have that during the long winter evenings. I remember one night everyone pitched in and shelled popcorn. Sis and Titter popped corn over the old wood-burning cook stove. They kept popping until they had popped enough to fill a washtub. We all sat around talking and eating popcorn until it was all gone, and we were all stuffed.

This small house which we rented was without electricity, had no running water, no phone and no indoor bath or toilet. We had no radio or daily newspaper. The only news we received was from conversation with other neighbors or from classmates at school. Almost all the news was bad anyway. Unemployment was at an all-time high; wages, if you were able to find work, were also very low. So perhaps not having a source for news was not so bad. We really didn't know how poor we were. Most of our neighbors were no better off than us. The farmers in the area, though they weren't making much money, were probably in a more prosperous situation than the folks living in the city. At least, they had food to eat.

Monday was wash day, and if the weather was "nice," this task was performed outside. After breakfast the top of the cook stove was full of buckets of water to be heated for the task. The hot water was carried outside and dumped into a large washtub. Another tub was filled with warm water for rinsing the washed clothing. Mom would gather all the dirty clothing and pile them up beside the washtub. The washboard was placed in the wash water. The first piece of clothing was soaked in the hot water and then rubbed with lye soap, which Mom had made, then rubbed up and down on the washboard, turning the piece of clothing as it was rubbed up and down on the board. More soap was added and more rubbing until the piece was clean. It was then put in the rinse water, and the soap water was removed by dashing the clothing up and down until all the soap had been removed. The item of clothing was rung out by hand and then put into a basket, ready to be hung on the clothesline. Sis and Titter helped Mom wash. As I look back, I don't know how Mom did it, washing clothing for ten people; it was a hard, back-breaking job. I'm sure the lye soap must have been hard on her hands. I remember as a child helping to carry water from the well to the kitchen on wash days, but as far as the work involved in washing the clothing, I was oblivious. All I knew was at the end of the day, we all had clean clothes to wear. We owned a washing machine after moving to Leavenworth, where we had electricity. It was a Maytag with a wringer for squeezing the water from the clothing. I don't know whatever happened to Mom's "old" washboard, but I'll bet Mom found an appropriate way to destroy it.

On occasion, Mom would send me with a few cents, 5 or 10, to a little filling station in Kickapoo to purchase kerosene for the lamps in the house.

****

During the winter of 1936 and 1937, Pop and my older brothers would cut wood to sell in Leavenworth. There were a lot of retired Army personnel who made their homes in Leavenworth. They would retire from Ft. Leavenworth and stay in the area. They received their Army pension, and while it wasn't very much, for the most part they were able to survive. They made good customers for the wood that Pop, Bud, France, Jim and on occasion, John and I would cut. John and I would go out when the weather wasn't terribly cold and help drag limbs, load wood and sack chips. The first thing that would take place upon arriving at the site where we were to cut was to build a fire. Next, Pop, Bud, France and Jim would select the trees to be cut and commence to chop and saw the trees down. Usually two or three were chosen and downed to start; we would then set about clearing the tree of all limbs and branches. The larger limbs were stacked to be cut later. The small branches would be cleared from the site and piled in huge brush piles.

Pop and Bud would start sawing the tree up; Pop would sharpen the saws every morning before we arrived for work. They were two-man crosscut saws. The sharp saw would make short work of sawing up the tree which usually was green and easy to saw.

France and Jim would relieve Pop and Bud on the saw from time to time. Sometimes it would be Bud and France on the saw, and Pop and Jim would relieve them. Those not sawing on the tree would begin splitting the wood. John and I would start to throw the split wood into the old pickup truck, which had been made from an old Packard automobile. The body of the Packard had been cut in half, just behind the front seat. The very rear of the body, which contained the rear window, had been cut off and moved forward to enclose the front cab of the truck. The bed of the truck was made from planks, and the side and tail end were made from heavy lumber. Sideboards were made and added to the bed so that it would hold about a rick of wood, or one-half a cord. By about 11 a.m., the pickup would be full. The tires would be pumped up with the hand pump to allow for the heavy load. We would all pile into and on the old truck and head to Leavenworth to sell the load before noon.

Pop had some regular customers that bought the wood on a regular basis. Some wood was used in heating stoves and some would be used in cook stoves. Cook stove wood would usually be cut smaller than heating stove wood. Pop would know ahead of time what size of wood the customers wanted. We would arrive at the customer's house and unload and stack the wood. Pop would collect the $1.00 for the load, and we would all pile onto the truck and head for the grocery store to buy lunchmeat or peanut butter for lunch. Peanut butter at that time was sold in bulk form, and the butcher would use a paddle to scoop the peanut butter into a meat carton. We would stop at the bakery and pick up the bread; three loaves of vienna bread for 10 cents. We would then head back to the work site, having spent 20 or 25 cents for our lunch.

Sometimes, when delivering wood, we would sell the cus-

28

tomer a large gunny sack full of chips for 25 cents. The chips were used to start the green wood. The chips we would gather were several days old and would be fairly dry. The 25 cents we received for the chips would pay for our lunch.

After arriving back at the work site, we would sit around the fire and eat our lunch. One of the grownups would slice the bread and pass it around and we would spread peanut butter on it, and that, to me, was the best meal you could ever hope for. On rare occasions, when we would sell an extra bag of chips, we would get six snowballs from the same bakery where we bought the bread. "Snowballs" were devils food cake filled with a white cream and rolled in coconut, just delicious! The cost for the six snowballs was 20 cents.

After eating, we would get back to work cutting the second load of wood. We would finish the second load just before dark. We then loaded all the tools onto the truck, and we all piled into the truck and headed for home. Upon arriving home, the water would have to be drained from the truck radiator and engine block so that it wouldn't freeze up the engine during the night. Anti-freeze was unheard of in those days. Alcohol was used then to prevent the radiator and block from freezing up, but if you had a leaky radiator, which we usually had, it was a waste of money buying alcohol. The battery was removed and carried inside so as to keep it warm in order to start the truck the next morning.

The following morning the battery would have to be installed; warm water was used to fill the radiator and the work day would start by delivering the load of wood on the truck to a customer. Then it was back to the woods to cut more wood.

Jim and myself were in school. When it was in session, we would be exempt from wood cutting, except for cutting wood for use at home. It took a lot of wood to warm the house using a large heating stove, and more wood was needed for

Pop, Bud, France, Jim, me, John. Circa 1935.

the kitchen cook stove. It was a never-ending battle. We were always glad when spring finally came and the weather would warm up. Then it was only necessary to cut wood for the cook stove. John had turned five in December and was still too young to go wood cutting on a regular basis.

****

After Christmas break, Jim, Titter and I started at the Kickapoo grade school. As I said earlier, our home sat at the bottom of a steep hill. On top of the hill sat the school. You could look from the windows of the one-room schoolhouse and see our house directly below.

Jim was one of two in the eighth grade. The other was Jimmy Newhouse. The Newhouse family was from Holland and they ran a dairy farm. Jim took me with him on one occasion to the Newhouse farm. I remember the smell of milk and cheese that permeated the whole house. The house was spotless and very clean, but I can still remember the aroma

30

of the milk and cheese.

Jim and Jimmy Newhouse were given the assignment of starting the fire in the coal furnace in the basement of the school. Jim would have to climb that hill early every school day, rain or snow. One Monday morning the hill was covered with a thick coating of ice. Jim tried to climb that hill but wasn't having much success. He would get part-way up and come sliding back down. He finally tied some cross links from an old tire chain around his feet and was able to make it up the hill. A short time later it was time for Titter and me to go to school. We fared no better than Jim in getting up the hill. We would get about halfway up, would lose traction and slide to the bottom of the hill. We would try again and again with the same results. What made it even worse, the whole school was looking out the windows at our fruitless and comical attempts, and we could see them all laughing. We finally walked around the hillside to a barbed wire fence and hand over hand we finally made it to school.

Mrs. Sharpe was the teacher for all grades in the one-room school. She also had a son, "Billy," who was in my class, which made a total of two in the first grade, both being named Billy. (I was called Billy by everyone until about the fourth grade. In my fourth grade class there was a girl by the name of Billie, so it was at that point I changed my name to Bill.) The teacher's son, Billy, sat in front of me in class. When Mrs. Sharpe would ask a question of me and I didn't know the answer, she would always ask her little Billy the same question and get the correct answer. I realized at that point I wouldn't have a chance of ever being tops in my class.

Mrs. Sharpe was married to a well-to-do farmer, and they had a nice farm in Kickapoo. I guess families like that came through the depression better than most. Bud and France worked for the Sharpe family from time to time.

One Saturday Bud took me along to spend the night with him on one of the farms he was working at the time. He was working for room and board. He had a nice room upstairs in the large farm house. The meal they served that Saturday evening was like a banquet to me: fried chicken, mashed potatoes and gravy, green beans and a lot of other items that we didn't have at home. They also served iced tea. I must have drank more iced tea at that supper than ever before. That evening, I went to the nice bedroom that Bud was using and climbed into the large bed with Bud. Sometime during the early morning hours, I awoke and had to do "number 1." I woke Bud and told him my problem. He grumbled and got up. I told him I couldn't make it to the outhouse. He grabbed a pot off the table and I went in it. It was then that Bud realized he had grabbed a flower pot with a hole in the bottom. Everything I put in the top came out the bottom, right onto Bud's bare feet. Needless to say, Bud never invited me to stay with him again.

Bud, being the oldest, didn't have much patience with the youngest siblings in the family. If we acted up around him or did something that he disapproved of, he would thump us on our heads and his knuckles could really sting you. It really hurt. I think that night in the bedroom he paid me back for soaking his feet.

****

France had an opportunity to apply for a job as an auctioneer at one of the large tobacco barns. They grew a lot of tobacco around Weston, and it was a good cash crop for the farmers in the area. It was cut and stored in huge tobacco barns until it was ready to sell. France had learned from our Uncle Crowe, who was an auctioneer, some of the tricks of auctioneering and thought he could handle the job. The owners of the large sales barn where farmers would bring tobacco to be sold gave France an audition, and he passed the test. He made good wages as an auctioneer, and I understand did an excellent job.

One Saturday morning in the fall of 1936, Bud volunteered to drive to St. Joe (St. Joseph) as Mom wanted to visit her sister and brother, Aunt Vernie and Uncle Roy. Pop and France were working and didn't get to go, but the rest of the family piled into Bud's big green Auburn with the big whitewall tires and headed to St. Joe. After a full day with our relatives, we were sailing along about halfway home when the right rear tire blew out. Bud was fighting the wheel trying to keep the big Auburn under control. We looked out the side windows and saw the big iron ring that held the tire to the wheel go flying past us. It jumped the fence and went several yards into the pasture that bordered the highway. Bud brought the Auburn to a stop, off the edge of the highway. Bud and Jim got out and surveyed the situation. Bud ordered all of us out of the car. With all of us standing along the highway, Bud began getting the tools out for changing the tire. The Auburn had a trunk hanging on the back of the car which held all the necessary tools. The spare tires were carried in wells on the front fenders. While Bud was jacking up the right rear, he told Jim to climb the fence and retrieve the big iron ring. Jim had just climbed through the barbed wire fence when a big bull came charging across the pasture. Jim retreated and climbed back through the fence. The bull was snorting and digging up the ground with its hoofs. Jim went running up the fence line for quite a distance yelling at the bull. Jim acted as if he was going to climb back into the pasture. The bull charged up the fence line towards Jim. While Jim kept the bull busy, Bud jumped the fence and retrieved the wheel ring. Bud and Jim finished changing the tire, and we headed home.

****

A family lived down from us, but a lot closer to the river. The road stopped at our house, so I don't know how they got to their house. I thought we were as far back as you could get, but it was kind of nice to know there was someone living even further in the sticks than us. I can't remember the family's name, but they had two boys who went to Kickapoo school. I remember they always smelled like cedar. I guess they burned cedar in their stoves. The older boy was in the fifth grade, I think. He had a double thumb on his right hand. I could not believe my eyes the first time I saw it. I didn't think it possible for someone to have three thumbs. I led a very sheltered life.

When we had lived at the Baskas farm during the harvest season of '36, Pop had worked for a farm family by the name of Wrenchlin (sp.?). It was a large family with six or seven boys and three or four girls. They were all big people and all worked the farm. It was a very nice farm and they did very well. During the harvest season farmers would help each other, cutting the wheat, shocking, thrashing and hauling the grain to the elevator. The thrashing machine would remain stationary, and the shocks or bundles of wheat would be carried to the thrashing machine by horse and wagon. The shocks of wheat would be fed into the thrasher. The grain would be discharged through a chute into a truck or wagon. The straw would be blown into a large straw stack. The thrasher was usually positioned wherever the farmer wanted the large straw stack to be. The straw would be used for many things, from cattle bedding, chicken houses and nests throughout the winter. Sometimes the straw would be baled and sold.

When the trucks were loaded, it would be hauled to the grain elevator and sold or placed in grainers on the farm to be sold at a later date. During harvest season, everyone was busy. Huge meals would be prepared by the women to feed the huge thrashing crews. All the farmers who had wheat wanted to get it harvested at about the same time and particularly if the weather was good. They wanted to get it to the elevators before the rain. Good "dry" wheat would bring more than wheat that had a high moisture content. Huge lines of grain trucks were evident at the grain elevators. The lines would continue throughout the harvest season. I would have the opportunity to work in a grain elevator in later years.

****

The reason for the digression to the late summer of '36 was to bring in the Wrenchlin family. The "large hill" I have mentioned before (our house in Kickapoo sat at the bottom of that hill) was an ideal hill on which to sleigh ride in the winter after a snowfall. One winter day after Christmas the ground was covered with about six or seven inches of snow. That afternoon and into the evening a large number of people, friends and neighbors, gathered for a sleigh riding party on the steep hill. A huge fire was built at the bottom close to our house, and everyone was sliding down the hill on sleds and anything else that would slide on snow, like pieces of tin, or scoop shovels; a few did have real sleds.

One of the younger Wrenchlin boys, about Sis' age and in high school with her in Leavenworth, was one of the group. I think he had a crush on Sis. He didn't have a sled, but did have a large grain scoop shovel which he was riding down the hill. He would sit on the scoop part with the handle in front. You would hold onto the handle and use it to steer. But there wasn't much steering a scoop shovel, and it pretty much went where it wanted to go. The young Wrenchlin boy came down the hill at a high rate of speed and was too close to the barbed wire fence (the one Titter and I used to get to school when the hill was a sheet of ice). The sleeve of his overcoat caught on the barbed wire fence. That fence ripped the sleeve off of his new overcoat. He was sick and embarrassed, ruining his new overcoat in front of Sis. Everyone else thought it was very funny but hid their laughter.

****

One Sunday that spring, Pop drove all of us to DeKalb in his big Packard automobile. It was a huge car with little jump seats in the back. It was probably a 1926 or 1927 model. One reason he had bought it was that all ten of us could fit into it. The roads in and around DeKalb were dirt, and some had a little gravel on them. The terrain around DeKalb is fairly hilly, and getting to Aunt Mildred (Pop's sister) and Uncle Sherman's farm in rainy weather was no easy thing. It had rained a day or so before we went, and the roads were muddy and slick. The Packard was a heavy car, and with all the family weighting it down, we did fairly well until we started down a very steep hill. Pop yelled for all to hold on as we started down. I don't think anyone was too scared until Pop yelled. The big Packard began to slide sideways as Pop applied the brakes to slow it down; we slid to the bottom sideways and had a wild ride. At the bottom, Pop and the older boys got out and spent some time trying to get the Packard lined up with the road again. We made it to our Aunt and Uncle's farm before noon.

Aunt "Mid", as we called her, was in the kitchen finishing up the huge meal when we arrived. The large wood-burning cook stove was filled with pots of food ready to be dished up. Fresh-baked pies were on the warming end of the stove. The water reservoir was used to heat about seven or eight

Pop's family, left to right: Pop, Annetta, Charles, Mildred, Paris and his wife, Maude

gallons of water, which was used to wash dishes, take baths and anything else for which hot water was needed. All water had to be carried in from the well outside, and the reservoir had to be filled each morning. Also, above the stove were warming ovens with doors to keep food warm.

Aunt Mid would usually bake three or four different pies: apple, peach and pumpkin or some other berry pie. We always looked forward to going to Aunt Mid and Uncle Sherman's house. They never had children, so they always treated us as their own kids. They really spoiled us. Uncle Sherman would always give John and I a "big" buffalo nickel. I say **big** because to us it looked the size of a silver dollar. After the huge meal and the kitchen was cleaned up, the adults would all retire to the living room and us "little ones" would play outside. Hide and seek was always fun. There were so many new places to hide. When we got tired of playing outside, we would go in and listen to the adults. Sometimes we would get the sterescope out and look at the 3-D views from around the world; the Eiffel Tower in Paris,

Yellowstone and Yosemite National Parks, World Fairs.

You would place a double picture in the little wire frame in front of the eye piece, then slide the picture in and out until it was focused. The picture would suddenly jump out in 3-D and you would almost think you were in those wonderful places. We would spend hours with the sterescope.

Around four o'clock, Pop would be ready to start home so as to get home before dark. Aunt Mid would not think of us leaving without fixing a small supper to eat before we left. It was usually about five o'clock when we left and dark when we arrived home. Aunt Mid and Uncle Sherman always made us feel special, and we thoroughly enjoyed our visits at their home.

Trips to visit our relatives in DeKalb or our aunts and uncles in St. Joe were usually made a couple of times a year. As gas was selling for about ten cents a gallon, it wasn't expensive and we really looked forward to those trips.

Other times, the family would make a trip to Uncle Charlie and Aunt Elva's farm for a Sunday visit. Uncle Charlie had a deep voice and was very articulate. They had two daughters, Mary Jo and Shirley June. After eating a large dinner, Mary Jo and Shirley June would entertain everyone by playing the piano and singing. I remember one song they would sing, and it went like this:

> *"Put on your old gray bonnet*
> *With the blue ribbon on it*
> *While I hitch old dobbin to the chaise,*
> *Through the fields of clover*
> *We will ride to Dover*
> *On our golden wedding day."*

Some of the other songs I remember are: "Silver Threads Among the Gold," "Blue Eyes," "I'll Take you Home Again" and "When You and I Were Young" (Maggie). They would also play and sing some religious songs, such as "The Sweet

Bye and Bye" and "Rock of Ages."

No one in our family would sing or could play the piano, so we always were impressed with the talents of our cousins.

On other Sundays, we would visit Pop's sister, Annetta, and Uncle Fred Dittamore. They were kind and gentle folks, and they had one son, Donald, and two daughters, Virginia and Margaret Lou. They were older than I, but we all got along great and always enjoyed our visits and great meals that Aunt Anetta prepared for us.

On Mom's side of the family was her sister, Aunt Vernie (who looked and sounded a lot like Mom), and Uncle Green Callaway, and Mom's brother, Uncle Roy, and Aunt Josephine. Aunt Vernie and Uncle Roy lived next door to each other, so it was easy to visit both when we made the trip to St. Joe.

There were a lot of cousins who matched up with our family in ages, so we always had someone to play with, or the older ones would go somewhere, such as Lake Contrary in South St. Joe, a large amusement park with rides. I was always too young to go, but Titter and Sis would go. Lake Contrary had an arcade, casino, theater, amusement park and race track and several hotels in its "hay day." The lake is still used for boating to this day.

****

One rainy Saturday in the spring, John and I were trying to find something to amuse ourselves. We discovered by climbing up on the headboard of Mom and Pop's bed, we could jump off onto the mattress and bounce a couple of times. We were jumping and bouncing when Mom came in and told us to stop before we hurt ourselves. When Mom left the room, as most kids, we decided to jump one more time. I climbed the headboard and really jumped hard. I hit the mattress and bounced head first onto the corner of the dresser. I hit on my left eyebrow and split my head open. A large flap of my forehead, just above my left eye, dropped down over my eye and was bleeding profusely. I ran to Mom in the kitchen, holding my eye with blood running between my fingers. Mom washed the blood off the cut and pulled the flap of skin up and pressed it back into place. Having no tape, Mom sent Titter up the hill to the Turpins' house to borrow some tape or a band-aid. Mom applied pressure until Titter got back with a band-aid. I probably should have had stitches, but the band-aid worked just fine, and a few days later it had healed up fairly well. It did leave a long scar just above my left eyebrow, which is there today. John and I never jumped from the headboard again.

Mom cooked big breakfasts and suppers every day for the family. She did her own baking, and at least one day a week was spent baking bread. She would bake several loaves at a time, enough to last all week, and she would bake biscuits just about every morning. They bought flour in 25-lb. cloth bags, which was dumped into a large metal can with a lid and was kept in the bottom of the kitchen cabinet. Mom would make dish towels from the flour sacks.

A typical meal at suppertime would be some type of meat, usually chicken in summer, or some type of pork meat, which was salt-cured in the fall, and kept through the winter in large barrels. Mom would open a quart of green beans or corn that she had canned during the summer, and we would have potatoes, mashed or fried, and gravy. She would make a light cream gravy and scramble a couple of eggs and stir into the gravy. It was delicious served over biscuits. We ate a lot of beans in the '30s. Mom would put in a hambone or some fried bacon for seasoning. I still like beans to this day. Mom had a way of making the most common foods taste special.

40

School came to an end for the year 1936-1937. Jim graduated and advanced to the 9th grade. All the graduating 8th graders from a number of one-room schools had a common ceremony at a one-room school several miles away. I remember the older family members going to the ceremony; John, Babe and myself stayed home. Titter was promoted to the fourth grade, and I would be a second grader in the fall. Sis would be a junior at Leavenworth Senior High.

On a clear, cold day in the fall, Pop would decide this was the day we would butcher a hog for our winter meat supply. Preparations would start by leaning a 55-gallon drum, with one end removed, at about a 45-degree angle on a stump or large rock, and filling with water. A fire was built around the drum to heat the water. While the water was heating, Pop would cut a green limb from an elm or hickory tree about 30 inches long and 3 inches in diameter. He would sharpen both ends of the limb and set it aside for later use.

An old barn door would be washed, cleaned and readied for use. When the water in the barrel was at the boiling point, Pop would get the 22 calibre rifle, and with one shot shoot the hog between the eyes. One shot would do the job. The hog was then bled by a sharp knife to the throat.

The hog was then slid into the drum of boiling water for just the proper amount of time, then removed and placed on the clean board. We would all begin scraping the hair from the hog using knives. The hair was easily removed and the hog was ready for the next step, which was to put cuts in the hind legs of the hog, revealing the tendons. The hickory or elm limb that Pop had prepared would be inserted between the hind legs of the hog with the sharpened ends of the limb inserted under the tendons. The hog would then be lifted to a hook hanging from the limb of a tree so that the hog was entirely off the ground. Pop would remove the head and cut the hog down the stomach, removing all the internal organs.

The hog was then washed down with hot water and allowed to cool for a short period of time.

The meat was then butchered, starting from the bottom, the shoulders, ribs, back bone and so on until the hams were hanging from the limb that had been used to hoist the hog up the hook on the tree.

The meat was allowed to "cool out" before packing it into barrels using curing salt. A layer of curing salt, a layer of meat, a layer of salt, then a layer of meat and so on until the barrel was full, at which time it was tightly sealed and left to cure.

Pop would always cut out the tenderloin to be eaten the first night at supper. Mom would prepare a meal which included the tenderloin in half-inch slices, fried, hot biscuits, mashed potatoes and gravy. What a meal! It made all the hard work of butchering worthwhile and besides we would have meat all winter.

CHAPTER 3

A Move to the City

THIS PRETTY MUCH ENDED our stay in Kickapoo, as the family was about to make the move to the city. (Before we leave Kickapoo, a sad note. We learned that my first grade teacher, Miss Muffin, who was a young single school teacher who lived alone in a small farm house not far from the Coffin school, had burned to death in her home which had caught fire from her kerosene cook stove. Seems she was preparing her evening meal on this stove when the fuel tank caught on fire, and in her attempt to extinguish the fire, the flames

Front: Bill, John and Babe

Back: Margaret Lou and Titter

ignited her clothing and she burned to death. It was a sad ending to our stay in Kickapoo.) During the summer of 1937 we packed up and moved to 112 Ottawa Street in Leavenworth, Kansas. Sis and Jim would be in high school, Bud and France were ready to find jobs in town, and it made sense to make this move. Pop rented a two-story house, about a half-block from the Esplanade. The Esplanade was a street that ran north and south with large, nice homes on just one side of the street. The homes overlooked a park that was on the other side of the street. From these homes, you could see the Missouri River below, as the Esplanade sat on very high ground. The Esplanade was home to many retired Army Officers from Fort Leavenworth and well-to-do families from Leavenworth.

The house Pop rented was first class as far as we were concerned. Indoor plumbing and electricity, had a large porch in front, and you could also walk out a door on the second floor onto a porch. It was a great place to sleep in the summer when it was hot inside. Pop paid $18 a month rent, which was more than we had paid anytime previously.

We had good neighbors on the east side, the McCalley's, with boys and girls our age, someone to play with at last. Mr. McCalley worked for the WPA (Works Progress Administration). He was a large man who always wore bib overalls. After Mr. McCalley finished work on Fridays, he would stop by the Court House and pick up a bag of fruit, vegetables, dry beans, lard and other food items that were given out to needy families. I was playing at the McCalley's house with Lonney McCalley, who was about my age, when Mr. McCalley arrived home from work one Friday. As usual, he had his bag of food items picked up from the Court House. In the bag were some oranges and I was given one. We could not afford to buy a lot of fruit, so I was delighted with the orange. I went home to show everyone the orange and told about the large bag of "free" food Mr. McCalley had brought home. Much to my amazement, Pop made me take the orange back. Pop seemed upset that I would take something without working for it and said we would not accept a handout from anyone. I didn't understand at the time, but did so in later years. Pop was a proud person and would not accept charity from anyone. It was his job, as head of the household, to see that we survived by hard work, and not handouts. As I look back, he did a pretty good job.

On the west side was our neighbor, Dwight Matthews, and his wife; they had no children, but were good neighbors. Mr. Matthews worked at the *Leavenworth Times*, the local newspaper. He helped Bud get a job as a "typesetter" shortly after we moved in. But, before Bud got the job at the *Times,* he worked the summer of 1937 for the railroad. His job was working at the Round-House across the Missouri River in Missouri. In the south part of Leavenworth, there was a railroad bridge that crossed the Missouri River and was used to send locomotives across the river to the Round-House where the engines were turned around, recrossed the bridge and headed in the opposite direction.

France took a job selling Hoover vacuum cleaners, and his job took him to Sedalia, Missouri, but he was home on weekends. Jim spent the summer with the CCC (Civilian Conservation Corps) and later got a job at Mehl & Schott's drug store located at Fifth and Delaware. Jim's job was to deliver prescriptions by bicycle. Their jobs did not happen overnight, as jobs were still scarce and it took a lot of perseverance and shoe leather to land a job in 1937. Younger people who wanted to work could usually find a job because they could be hired for a very small wage. The minimum wage at that time was $.25/hour. That was $2 a day, twice as much as they were earning working for farmers.

Directly across the street on the south side lived the

Titter, Babe,
Bill and John
112 Ottawa St.
1937

Whitman family. They had a daughter, Dorothy, about the age of Titter, and they became very good friends.

Sis was still in high school and Jim started high school. Titter, John and myself began school that fall at North Broadway school, which was about ten blocks from home. In good weather we walked to school. In the winter when the weather was really bad, snow or bitter cold, Pop or France would drive us to school. No school buses in those days. We would take our lunch in a paper sack or wrapped in newspaper. Some kids brought their lunch in Karo Syrup buckets. The bucket was metal and held about two quarts of syrup. The bucket had a wire handle and a snap-on lid, which made an ideal lunch bucket. Mom always made our syrup when we had pancakes, so we didn't buy Karo Syrup; therefore, we never got the bucket for carrying my lunch. A usual lunch would consist of a peanut butter sandwich and sometimes a piece of fruit or homemade cake. Sometimes the sandwich would contain a potted meat which was a real treat. There was a small corner grocery store a short distance from school. Sometimes if we had a nickel, we could get a bowl of soup. The owner had a couple of small tables, and a few of the kids would go there for lunch. The soup always came with a good supply of those little oyster crackers which were new to me, and I would fill up on those little crackers.

Pop was still working for farmers in the Kickapoo area. He drove a grain truck for a man by the name of Gwartney. He must have liked Pop's work, as he usually had a job of some sort for Pop.

The winter of '37 brought a huge snowfall to our area. I remember we had a great time playing in the snow. Pop would haul wood home from his job in Kickapoo. Usually, it was in the form of logs about ten feet long, and we would saw it up in our backyard. John and I would help Pop saw it up into firewood.

We were always amazed at the ease Dwight Matthews' car would start on cold winter mornings. He had a fairly new Ford automobile, and it always started in the morning. The old cars we had would always give Pop, Bud and France problems, such as dead batteries and frozen radiators. We had no garage, so the cars would set out in the snow and cold. Family car owners would start early in the morning getting the cars started, and once they started, would leave them running until time to leave for work. We weren't the only ones on the block who had problems. You could see car owners up and down the street struggling to get their transportation started and putting on tire chains, except for Dwight Matthews. He also had a garage.

Spring finally came and the hardships of winter gave way to a more tranquil way of life. Pop would always plow up a portion of the backyard for a garden. Potatoes, sweet corn, green beans and many other vegetables would be planted. Mom would always can the excess vegetables for winter use.

Bud and France always gave Mom part of the money they earned so she had a few extra dollars for household expenses.

There were several children in the neighborhood who would meet to walk to school. We would pass a home with a large screened-in porch. On this porch a huge dog was kept,

47

John and Bill
112 Ottawa Street, 1937

and he would bark wildly at the group as we passed the house. I don't recall us ever trying to antagonize the dog, as he was huge and we wanted no part of him. On this particular morning he began his frantic barking act, and we hurried to get past the house. He was jumping against the screen, and suddenly the screen gave way and he charged at us. We all started running and I don't know why but he chose my rearend to bite, and he sank his teeth into my little butt, and it was only with the help of my fellow walkers and, finally, the owner of the dog, that he was forced to release me. We walked on to school and I sat on my left cheek all day.

I told Mom what had happened when we got home from school, and they called the doctor to come to the house that evening and he doctored it. I never saw the wound because it was in a place I couldn't see. I guess the dog wasn't rabid because I recovered in a short time. We took a different route to school after that.

If you went down the alley behind our house, you would walk behind the back yard of a house that faced the street to the west of Ottawa, our street. In the back yard of that house was a large dog that was kept on a chain. There was no fence and the chain was not long enough for the dog to reach the alley. We would walk that way from time to time and the dog would bark and try to get at us, but the chain prevented him from reaching us. One day the daughter of Arden Ryan, a well known policeman for the City of Leavenworth who lived in the area, was walking down the alley, and the dog, chained in the back yard, began his barking and tugging at his chain trying to get at the girl. Suddenly the chain snapped and the dog attacked the little girl and really mauled her. If it had not been for the owner pulling the dog off, the little girl would probably have been killed. When her father learned of the attack, he promptly dispatched the dog with his service revolver. The alley was safe to use after that day.

****

Arden Ryan was well liked by everyone and much admired by the young boys. He rode a "big" Harley and had the black boots and white helmet and really looked the part of a law enforcement officer. He led all the parades in town and every funeral procession. The young boys all wanted to be motorcycle cops.

Speaking of parades, every Armistice Day, November 11th, there was a parade in downtown Leavenworth. High school bands and R.O.T.C. units and other civic groups participated, and Fort Leavenworth would be well represented with the Army Band, Cavalry units and Artillery units. To a young boy, these parades were a highlight. I can still remember standing on the sidewalk or sitting on the curb watching the parade. It would start with Arden Ryan coming down Delaware, the main street, on his "big" white Harley with siren and red lights flashing, weaving back and forth across Delaware keeping the spectators on the sidewalks and out of the street. The parade began at 11 a.m., the exact time the Armistice was signed ending the 1st World War. The local high school bands would usually be the lead unit with the R.O.T.C. units close behind. The mayor and other city leaders and the commanding officer from Fort Leavenworth would ride by in open top cars. Down the street, over and above the sound of the high school band and bands from the surrounding communities you could hear the U.S. Army band playing "Stars and Stripes" and drowning out the other bands. The Army band always looked so sharp. The band would be followed by a horse cavalry unit. The horses were always groomed and, with their black bridles and cavalry saddles with big brass "U.S." buttons, would open the eyes of a small boy sitting on the curb. The Mounted Cavalry unit would be followed by the horse-drawn artillery pieces with their caisson behind.

Another event the family enjoyed was the 4th of July. We would all load into the car and drive to the Old Soldier's home at Wadsworth, which was located just south of Leavenworth. It was a hospital for American Veterans, mostly from the 1st World War. On the 4th of July, the Veterans Band would put on a concert. The band itself would be seated on the bandstand, and the visitors would bring their own chairs or blankets and sit on the grass. The band would play John Phillip Sousa's marches and other patriotic songs.

Living in town offered much more to do than living on the farm. On Saturdays John and I would go out and collect pop bottles and turn them in at Doran's grocery store, a small neighborhood store a couple of blocks from our house. We would receive two cents a bottle. We then used the money to go to the movie which cost ten cents. If we had a good day of finding pop bottles, we could also buy popcorn which was five cents. It was on one of these trips to the movies on a summer Saturday afternoon that Titter, John and I decided to see the first feature a second time. (For a ten-cent admission to the movies, you saw two full feature films, a cartoon and a serial which ended each time with a cliff hanger in order to get you back the following week.) I don't remember the film, but we must have liked it because we stayed and watched it a second time.

Usually, we would leave the theater about 4:30 p.m. or so and walk home, arriving about 5:00 p.m. Because we saw the first feature twice, it was after 6:00 p.m. when we left the theater. Unknown to us, a tornado was approaching Leavenworth from the southwest. As we started home, it began to rain, the wind picked up and while we were still only halfway home, the tornado hit. Trees were being blown over and large limbs were snapped off. The rain was coming down in sheets, lightning was flashing all around. Titter, John and I trudged on, holding onto fences lining the sidewalk. By the time we reached home, the worst of the storm had passed. Mom and Pop were frantic as they thought for sure we had been blown away. Pop was in the act of driving to the theater to check on us when we walked into the house, dripping wet. We were scolded for leaving the theater so late *and during a tornado*. I think they were just relieved we were home.

Our family never had a refrigerator, always an ice-box. As an ice-box required ice to do its job of keeping and preserving foods, we would have to purchase ice on a regular basis. One problem with an ice-box was the ice we put in it would eventually melt, and a "pan" was necessary to catch the water. There was a hose or pipe which led from the ice compartment in the top of the ice-box to the bottom and through the bottom of the ice-box. A pan was placed under the ice-box to catch the melted ice. Any time the family would be gone for the day, the "drip pan" would have to be emptied just before we left to prevent the run-over and soaking of the floor while we were gone. Now, when a family leaves the house for a trip, someone will always ask, "Did you turn off the coffee pot?" Then, it was, "Did you empty the drip pan?"

51

The ice man in our area drove a one-horse wagon, a huge box on wheels that would hold a large amount of 300-pound blocks of ice. The ice man, using an ice pick, would chisel off the amount of ice according to the cardboard sign hanging in the front room window of a home. The card could be hung four different ways with the amount of ice required at the top; 10, 15, 25 and 50 lbs. Ice was not expensive, but was required almost daily, so it was a constant drain on the household food budget. Ten cents a day would probably have to be allotted for ice. A large chunk of ice was needed for the weekend. Ice water, ice tea and ice for an occasional bottle of "pop" would put a large dent into the block of ice.

The ice man's horse would know the route as well as the ice man himself and would walk from house to house and stop. Water was always dripping from the wagon, and the ice man would give the kids playing in the area the small broken chips of ice. We would always be at the rear of the wagon while he was chipping off the needed piece of ice, hoping a mistake would be made and we would profit from that error.

Farm produce was also sold from a horse and wagon. Every morning, some time before noon, a farmer driving a wagon loaded with fruit and vegetables, in season, would go house to house selling his wares. We always had a garden, so would only buy things we did not grow.

There were quite a number of farmers still driving horses and wagons. Downtown at Sixth and Cherokee, on the southeast corner, there was a large area known as "Hay Market Square." This was the area where farmers sold their produce, as well as hay. There was a large concrete watering trough where farmers could water their horses and leave their teams and wagons while they did their shopping. It was a busy place on Saturdays as this was the day most people made the trip to town, some from quite a distance.

Mom would send John and me to Doran's corner grocery store to buy something she needed to fix lunch or supper. The smell of that small corner grocery store is one you can never forget, and once in a while you get a whiff of that smell upon entering a small country store to this day. It's an unforgettable aroma!

We could buy a small loaf of bread for a nickel and enough lunch meat, which was sliced in front of your eyes, for ten cents, to feed lunch to all of us. I remember Mom giving us the "mill" or two that was required for the state tax. A mill was 1/1000 of a dollar, and they came in 1, 5, 10 and 25 denominations and were made of aluminum. If you had no mills for tax, the clerk would charge a penny and give you back your change in mills. We made a lot of trips to Doran's over the years we lived on Ottawa Street.

When France was home on weekends, he would buy bananas by the stalk at the market in Kansas City and sell them door to door. France was a good salesman and never had a problem selling all of his bananas. He did all right selling Hoover vacuum cleaners, too, but I think he disliked driving to Sedalia, Missouri every week. He took a job with Montgomery Ward selling tires on commission. The store manager was glad to do this, as no salary would have to be paid. France would surprise the store manager by selling so many tires, his commission would be larger than the salary of the manager. He would see cars on streets with bald tires, would get their license number and check at the Court House for their address. He would then call on them to see if they would like to buy new tires.

I think it was 1938, while listening to the radio one evening, we learned that *Martians* were invading earth. The broadcast was so realistic that whole families were seen standing outside looking up, afraid of what they might see, including our family. It was a regular program on the radio,

Back: Vernard Dykes, Sis, Ruth Walker and Bud.

Front: Friend of Ruth with Cleda Dykes. Circa 1938.

with announcers breaking in every few minutes with up-
dates on the advancement of the Martians as they were observed on a farm in New Jersey.

The older members of the family — Bud, France and Sis
— were not home, probably had dates, and Pop kept saying,
"I wish they were home so we could all leave together." Pop
had a plan of finding a cave along the Missouri River where
we might fight off the Martians and survive.

When the truth came out that Orson Welles had pulled
one over on millions of Americans, Pop said he thought it
was all a fake. But I remember seeing his face as he looked
skyward that evening. He was sure we wouldn't survive
such a menace.

Jim was delivering prescriptions and other items, by bicycle, for Mehl and Schott's drug store. I think it was the
summer of 1938, when Jim was involved in an accident. It
seems a car had struck the bike Jim was riding, and Jim
suffered a broken arm and scrapes and bruises.

Leavenworth was home for some coal mines that were in the south end of town and along and under the Missouri River. The miners walked home from work in the late afternoon, and we would see them pass by with their carbine lamps on their helmets. They would be covered with coal dust. Eventually the mines would extend so far under the river that they became unsafe and too expensive to operate, so they were closed down some time later.

In the summer of 1939, Bud was married to Ruth Walker. It was a big occasion, as Bud was the first to leave the family. With Bud's help, John and I were dressed in new white pants and white shoes for the wedding. Ruth Walker's father was a guard at the Federal Prison in Leavenworth. He was known by the inmates as "Old Iron Jaw." With "Old Iron Jaw's" help, Bud was able to get on as a guard at the Prison in 1940 and would become known by the inmates as "Little Iron Jaw." Bud and Ruth rented a house next door to Ruth's mother and father on Ottawa Street.

Sis was going with Vernard Dykes, who worked at the DeCoursey Dairy bottling plant on North Fifth Street. DeCoursey had an ice cream drive-up store on North Fifth Street, adjacent to the plant. The drive-up store was built of

Left:
Bill and John,
Aunt " Mid"
and Babe
in background

Right:
Pop and Mom

Bud's wedding
day, 1939

glass blocks. Everyone called it the "glass house," and Pop would take us there once in a while on Saturday evenings and buy us a cone, a double dip for a nickel. We all looked forward to this trip.

A couple of times a year, the DeCoursey Dairy would clean out their ice cream lockers and get rid of all outdated ice cream. Vernard, being an employee, would take all the outdated ice cream he wanted. On Saturday evening he came to pick up Sis for a date and brought several half-gallons of ice cream. There was no vanilla, chocolate or strawberry flavors we liked, only odd flavors such as lemon, pistachio, raspberry and some other unfamiliar flavors. We ate and ate all we could hold and threw away the leftovers, as we had no way of preserving it. An ice-box would not keep ice cream frozen! For once, we all had our fill of ice cream.

One day during the late summer of '39, there came a knock at the front door of our house. Mom answered the door and saw a small older man standing there, hat in hand. He asked Mom if she could spare something to eat. This was not an unusual request as we lived not far from the Missouri Pacific Railroad tracks, which ran along the Missouri River, and almost daily some "down-on-their-luck" bum who had ridden the "rods" and gotten off at Leavenworth would knock at the back door wanting to split wood or hoe the garden for something to eat. Mom told the old man standing at the front door to go around to the back door, and she would try to find something to eat. The old man looked at Mom with tears in his eyes and said, "Beulah, I'm your father." Mom was dumbfounded. She had not seen her father for 37 years, not since she was 8 years old. They embraced and Mom asked Grandpa to come in. Grandpa said he was not alone. He stepped to the sidewalk and waved to a car parked down the street. Out stepped Mom's sister and brother, Aunt Vernie and Uncle Roy (Minnie had died at an early age). Seems Grandpa had retired from the Atchison, Topeka & Santa Fe Railroad in Topeka, Kansas, and decided to look up his children. He started in St. Joseph, as that was the last known location of the family. He located Uncle Roy, having the same last name, and who worked for the Burlington Northern Railroad. It was no problem finding Aunt Vernie as she lived next door to Uncle Roy.

Titter, John, Babe and myself had all been out playing and came home to a house full of company and a new Grandpa. Mom fixed supper for the group, and one by one the rest of our family came home from work and met Grandpa for the first time. It seems Grandpa had remarried, and when his second wife died, he decided to find his children.

A few weeks later Grandpa summoned Mom and Pop to St. Joe, along with Aunt Vernie and Uncle Roy. Seems Grandpa had been very thrifty through the years and was able to present each of his children a large amount of cash. A large amount for 1939, $3,500. When Mom and Pop arrived home from St. Joe, they allowed all of the kids to hold the huge wad of cash. Never had we seen so much money! Mom and Pop spent the money wisely. They bought a house and three acres on the west edge of Leavenworth, 320 South 11th Street.

The owners of the house we were renting (on Ottawa Street) had a chance to sell the house, so we moved to a house on Ohio Street for a month or so while waiting for closing on our "new" home. While living in the Ohio Street home, we were enrolled in school for the 1939-1940 school year. We went to Franklin School for only a short time. We moved to 320 South 11th Street late in the fall of 1939. After this move, we were enrolled at Maplewood School. It was an old school, but was within walking distance from home, about six or seven blocks. We had neighbors with children our age, some in the same class as Titter, John, Babe and me.

CHAPTER 4

Family's First (Owned) Home

THE "NEW" HOME was anything but new. It was a two-story house with wood siding. It had a large kitchen, dining room and living room downstairs. There were three bedrooms upstairs. On the back of the house, behind the kitchen, there was a room with a sloping roof. It was used as a laundry room and storage. There were stairs in this room that led to the basement. The basement was only partially finished. The house was wired for electricity, but had no indoor plumbing.

First Owned Home — 320 South 11th Street
Circa 1942.

There was an outhouse and a well for our water. The three-acre pasture made a perfect place to play baseball, football and other games. There was a small barn. Pop bought a cow for milk shortly after we moved in. It was John and me who were given the job of milking it morning and night. We also had chickens for eggs and eating.

France was still working at Montgomery Ward and got a good deal on a new refrigerator. He surprised Mom with it, and I guess it was the first refrigerator we ever had. No more "ice box" and emptying the drip pan. Now all we needed was something to put in the new refrigerator.

The "new" house sat on a gravel street and at the top of a steep hill. Seems we never lived on flat ground, and even when we lived in Beverly the ground there was more water than dirt. This hill did allow us a way of getting our car started in the winter. If the battery was low and wouldn't start the car, you would roll down the hill and put the car in low gear and let the clutch out. Most times, the car would start somewhere down the hill. If the car didn't start by the time you reached the bottom of the hill, you had a real problem.

Our barber lived about halfway down the hill on the right. I don't recall their name, but they sold Watkins products and had a sign on their fence that stated such. Pop would take John and me down every three or four months for a haircut. It was usually after supper when we went, and the barber's stomach would growl all during the haircutting process. Your head would be next to his stomach, and while a radio would have been better, at least we had something to occupy our time. I think the haircut cost 15 cents apiece. I believe at that time the going price for a haircut in a barber shop was 25 cents.

At the bottom of that hill on the corner of South 11th and Cherokee Streets was a small corner grocery store. Over the years it played a big part in our daily routine. We would sell Mom's homemade butter and eggs from our chickens to the grocer. We bought items from him when we ran out between trips to A&P, Big Jumbo and Kroger's downtown. In the summertime, we would make trips down the hill to buy a bottle of pop or to buy lunch meat for summer lunches. Mom would bake almost all our bread and pastries, but once in a while we would be forced to buy store bread. We always liked store bread, not because it was better, but because it was different.

Grandpa, now that he had found his children, would spend time living with each one. It was always nice having Grandpa with us. We would make trips down the hill to the corner grocery to buy his George Washington pipe tobacco. The tobacco cost 10 cents, but he would usually give us an extra nickel, which we spent on candy or pop. Mom never allowed smoking in the house, but made an exception for Grandpa. I guess it was because it was his monetary gift that made the house possible. Besides, between the wood-burning cook stove and the big heating stove, both put a lot of smoke into the house every time you opened the stove door. I guess the little George Washington smoke didn't make much difference.

Grandpa was sitting by the pot belly stove one day puffing on his pipe, and told John and me a story about the early days in St. Joseph, Missouri. He said there were several freight lines that hauled freight to and from St. Joe and Kansas City. This was before motorized trucks, and all freight was hauled by huge freight wagons, pulled by large draft horses.

Grandpa told of one such trip. A wagon load of freight left St. Joe headed for Kansas City early one cold winter morning. The skies were gray and covercast and looked like it could snow. The temperature began to drop, and it did begin to snow. Blizzard conditions bore down on the freight wagon. The teamster continued on toward his destination. The teamster had a jug of whiskey on the seat beside him and would take a long drink ever so often to fight off the cold. The teamster would stick his thumb in the neck of the jug to keep it from splashing out.

It was late in the afternoon when the wagon load of freight pulled into the terminal in Kansas City. The team of horses were exhausted. They were covered with snow and ice, and huge bellows of steam were pouring from their nostrils. The terminal station master came out to check in the freight and saw the teamster sitting up, covered with ice and snow, stiff as a board. He had frozen to death, all but his thumb, which was still stuck in the whiskey jug.

That summer or late fall, Pop told John and me that we would have to lead our milk cow, "Daisy," out to the Wiley farm at 20th and Spruce Streets. Pop wouldn't tell us it was to get Daisy bred, but would tell us that Daisy was "bulling." Wileys had a big "white face" bull and Pop had made arrangements for Daisy to be at their farm to meet their bull. John and I led Daisy by a rope tied around her horns, about two miles or so, to the Wiley farm. Daisy would be turned into the pasture with the bull. John and I would be free to wander around the farm. The Wileys had two daughters, and one of them was in my class. I was too bashful to talk with her very much, but she was nice enough to show us around. After a while, Mr. Wiley said Daisy was ready to go home, so we attached the lead rope and walked her home. Seems Daisy always walked more slowly going home.

Sis graduated from high school in 1939. She landed a job at the National Hotel at 4th and Cherokee Streets. Sis worked in the hotel dining room as a waitress. She was a good waitress and did well with tips. Most tips were 10 to 25 cents. On July 12, 1940, she was married to Vernard Dykes. A regular customer at the dining room, a man who knew she was about to get married, left a dollar tip with a congratulations note. A dollar tip was unheard of, and Sis told the whole family of his generosity.

Sis married into a family even larger than ours, while there were 10 in our family, I think the Dykes family contained 12. Vernard had a sister, Freda, who would become a Williams in 1941.

In the fall of 1940, John and I started at Maplewood school. I was a fourth grader; John was in the third grade. Our teachers were sisters by the name of Emma and Grace Keiser. They were neighbors of ours. Grace taught the third grade and Emma the fourth. John's classroom was on the north side of school and faced our house, although you could not see our house. We were some seven or eight blocks from school. One morning while John was sitting at his desk, he happened to look out the window and saw Daisy, our cow, looking back at him from the school yard. He pretended not to see Daisy as he was too embarrassed. The teacher, Ms. Keiser, saw Daisy about this time and asked the students if anyone knew who owned the cow. John was forced to admit that the cow belonged to him. He was excused from class to take Daisy home.

Some afternoons while walking home from school, I would be confronted by Billy Zink. The Zink family lived down the street from us, and Billy and his brother, Edwin, would walk the same route as me. Billy would start a fight with me, and brother Edwin would join the fight ,and I'd find myself fighting both, and sometimes even their sister would join in. I don't know what their problem was, but did know their home life wasn't the best. Sometimes John would come along and help me. Between the two of us, we could pretty much hold our own.

In our home, Mom and Pop's bedroom was at the top of

the stairs and to the left. Mom and Pop would usually retire early to listen to the 9:00 p.m. news on their bedside radio. The news in the '40s was mostly about the war in Europe. The newscasters at that time were Gabriel Heater, Edward R. Murrow and Walter Winchell. I guess there were others, but these three men seemed like members of the family as they were our contact with the outside world. When Mom and Pop went to bed at night, the kids would stay up awhile and listen to the big Philco radio in the dining room. Some of the programs we listened to during the evening were Fibber McGee and Molly, Amos and Andy, Jack Benny, The Green Hornet and Intersanctum. There were others, Bob Hope and lots of "Big Band" music and the Hit Parade. You had to use your imagination a lot, but the sound effects made it possible to see with your ears. You always knew what would happen when Fibber McGee opened the hall closet door. We would get to listen to Jack Armstrong sometimes when we got home from school, if our chores were done.

In the summer of 1941 Pop decided to go to western Kansas to work in the wheat harvest. Jim and his friend, Clyde Dykes, brother of our brother-in-law, Vernard, told Pop that they would like to go with him and work the harvest. Jim owned a 1934 Ford convertible coupe and said he would drive. Jim and Clyde only had a few dollars for the trip, which left Pop to pay most of the expenses: gas and food. Pop was so disgusted with Jim and Clyde because on their first stop for gas, they both blew most of their money for sunglasses. Pop was forced to pay for the gasoline. After the first week or so, Jim and Clyde grew tired of the heat, dust and long hours in the wheat field. They received their paycheck and took off for Leavenworth, leaving Pop alone to work the harvest. Pop would send his wages home to Mom, and once he enclosed four dollars, one each for the younger ones. We were very excited about having a whole dollar of our own. When the wheat harvest ended in Kansas, Pop had to take the bus home.

Pop traded in his Model A Ford for a 1935 Chrysler Air Flow; the car claimed to be ahead of its time. By the time Pop bought it, the rest of the automobile industry had caught up with it, so the Chrysler Air Flow looked a little odd with the sloping hood. It was light brown in color and really rode nice, compared to the Model A. I recall when Pop decided to trade, the Model A wasn't running, so Pop devised a plan to get the Model A to the dealer's lot so as to make the dealer think the Model A was in running condition. The Model A was towed to a hill which ran toward and past the car dealer. Pop got in the Model A and rolled downhill and coasted into the dealer lot and traded it for the Chrysler Air Flow. Pop thought he had put one over on the car dealer, but the car dealer had the last laugh because the Chrysler Air Flow had starter problems and would not start every time, which made the hill we lived on invaluable.

One evening Pop came home from work in his old pickup, an old Chevy coupe with a homemade bed on the back, to find his Chrysler missing from its usual parking place. He knew at once who had it — Jim. Jim had done this before, borrowed his car without permission. Pop took off to look for his car and driver. He drove to the main street, Delaware, and parked. He guessed correctly. It wasn't long before he spotted his car coming down Delaware. Jim was driving with Clyde Dykes by his side. Pop ran out into the path of Jim, waving his arms for Jim to stop. Jim saw Pop in the middle of Delaware waving his arms and, without stopping, Jim jumped out, with Clyde doing the same, leaving the car continuing down the street, knowing Pop would be forced to stop the car rather than chase them. I think Jim stayed with Clyde at his house that night, giving Pop time to cool down.

In the early part of 1941, the news wasn't very good when

it came to world events. The Japanese were fighting in China and committing atrocities that shocked Americans. Germany had taken over most of Europe and was in the process of defeating England.

In 1940, President Roosevelt was elected to a third term. He gave 50 of our old World War One destroyers to England. Some in Congress and the public weren't too keen about getting involved in another European war. Only some 20 years had passed since Americans had helped Europe fight the 1st World War, the war to end all wars. So a lot of Americans and many in Congress thought that the giving of 50 American destroyers to England was in itself an *act of war*.

Not long after this, the first peace time draft act went into effect, and on October 29, 1940, the first numbers were drawn. The President said that the reason for the draft was for the defense of American shores. The President also said that no American boy would be sent to war in Europe.

In 1940 and 1941, the pressure kept building like an overinflated inner tube covered with patches. I am giving the above history only to show the attitude of most Americans in regard to war.

When school ended in May, we were told that the old Maplewood School would be torn down to make room for a new school and that we would all be attending the junior high school the following year while the new school was being built. The junior high school was quite a ways further from home and would require a much longer walk come September, but summer was here and we would worry about all this come fall.

During the summer I had my first fountain coke. France was still selling tires for Montgomery Ward and had gotten married in April to Freda Dykes. One day in June, France had an appointment to see a farmer in Winchester, a small town north and west of Leavenworth. Freda was going with

France, and they invited me to go with them. I was excited and jumped at the opportunity. We drove to the farm in Winchester, and France talked to the farmer about new tires for his truck. Freda and I waited in the car and watched as France, with his foot resting on the bumper of the truck with the bald tires, sold the farmer a new set of tires. We saw them shake hands, and France returned to the car with a slight smile on his lips. France celebrated the sale by stopping at the drug store in Winchester and buying us a fountain coke. We sat on tall stools at the soda fountain and drank our cokes. I still remember how good that coke tasted with all that shaved ice. It's one of those moments in time when you can recall all the details.

We had a small barn behind our house on South 11th Street where we kept feed for the cow and also a stall where we milked Daisy. On the end of the barn was a small chicken house. Early every spring, Pop would order 50 to 100 baby chicks through the local feed store. We would pick them up when they came in. We always had a spot prepared for them in the large store room behind the kitchen. We used large cardboard boxes and would hang a large light bulb directly over the box and at just the right height. At night, the baby chicks would spend more time under the light to keep warm. But I don't think they slept very much. The feeders where we put the feed needed our constant attention as those small chicks ate constantly, and fresh water was another thing that kept us busy. Washing the watering jars and filling them was an ongoing chore. The chicks grew fast, and it wasn't long before they began to sprout feathers, and by June they were large enough to begin butchering. Fried chicken was a staple meat during the summer. The roasters were eaten, and the hens were kept for eggs. Mom fried chicken several times a week, and it was usually my job to kill the chicken and pick the feathers, after they had been dipped in scalding water.

On the other end of the barn was a pen where we kept a couple of hogs for butchering come fall. There was a small area between the cow barn and the hog shed where the feed was kept for all the animals. Pop was going to pour a step outside the back door of the house, so he bought a couple bags of cement and stored it in the feed room in the barn until he had time to pour the step. A few weeks went by, and one morning when I went to the barn to milk Daisy, I went to the feed room to get grain for her and found both pigs dead. The grain for the cows had been eaten and the bags of cement had been torn open and most of it was gone. Seems the hogs had broken into the feed room and had made "pigs" of themselves. They were "stone" dead. The cement they had eaten set up, and they were both hard as rocks. There went our winter meat supply and our back porch step. We buried the hogs in the far corner of the pasture, and I guess they are still there and will be until sometime in the future when some archaeologist digs them up.

The summer was filled with cutting weeds and hoeing in the garden, cutting wood for our wood-burning cook stove, milking and caring for our chickens. We had an old reel-type lawnmower that you pushed. Our lawn was made up of mostly weeds, and what the reel mower wouldn't cut, we used a hand sickle to try and keep the weeds from getting too high.

As the summer heat increased in July and August, we would sleep out in the yard on blankets to escape the heat in our bedrooms. We had no air conditioning and no insulation in the walls or roof of our house. The summer heat would build up in our upstairs bedrooms, and it became almost impossible to sleep. Mom and Pop had a small fan in their bedroom. It was the only fan in the house. If it started to rain during the night, we would move to the screened porch along the south side of the kitchen. It was really nice sleeping in the yard. Not only was it much cooler than inside, there was a line of tall poplar trees that we slept under, and the breeze blowing through the trees would create a soothing, rustling sound in the leaves that would lull you to sleep.

On Saturdays, if we could get the 10 cents, we would walk to town, about a mile or so, and see a double feature movie. Charlie Chan and Sherlock Holmes were always good. The westerns with Roy Rogers, Gene Autry, and Tom Mix were also a weekly fare. Everyone knew Champion was Gene Autry's horse and Trigger was Roy's horse.

In 1941 jobs were still hard to come by in the Midwest, but in some of the large manufacturing cities jobs were becoming a little more plentiful. America was shipping a lot of war material to Europe, and a lot of factories were producing this type of lend-lease material.

In September 1941 we all started to school at the Third Avenue Junior High School. I was in the fifth grade, and John was in the fourth grade. Titter was already in junior high by this time. It was about two miles or so to school, which meant we would have to get up a lot earlier in order to get our chores done, milking, etc., and get to school on time. It was exciting to be going to a junior high school with all the seventh, eighth and ninth graders. We still had only one teacher and one room for our schooling, while the junior high aged students went to different rooms for their classes, but it was different. We took our lunches every day and went to the gymnasium and sat on the bleachers to eat.

As mentioned earlier, our old Maplewood school was being torn down to make room for a new school, which was to be completed for classes the following year.

CHAPTER 5

The War Years — The Depression Ends

THE NEXT EVENT I remember came on a Sunday afternoon in December 1941. I was outside getting water from the well. Titter came out the back door and told me that it had just come over the radio that the Japanese had bombed Pearl Harbor. I don't recall being shocked or too excited. I had no idea where Pearl Harbor was, but went inside and heard the reports coming in over the radio. It seems the newscasters would keep breaking in on the regular programming with bits and pieces of news all afternoon. Before the day was over, I knew where Pearl Harbor was and why the attack was so vital to America. I remember hearing the President talking to Congress on radio and also the next day when Congress declared war on the Empire of Japan. Things were happening fast. A short time later (three days) Germany and Italy declared war on the United States, and suddenly we were up to our necks in war, and our lives would be changed forever.

A short time after December 7th, Jim enlisted in the Army. I remember going down to City Hall and on the front steps seeing Jim being sworn into the Army, along with a large number of other young men from the area. We all hated to see Jim leave home, but were very proud of him.

Leavenworth suddenly became a very busy place, with Fort Leavenworth becoming one of the major receiving centers for men volunteering and being drafted into the Army. New recruits were arriving daily by trains and buses. All this activity didn't quickly relate to more people downtown and on the streets of Leavenworth, because as soon as the new recruits were given physicals and screened, they were shipped out to other Army camps for basic training. We did see an increase in the number of Army personnel stationed at Fort Leavenworth to administer to the large influx of new recruits.

I have forgotten where Jim took his basic training, but remember he went to a tank destroyer school in Texas after basic training. He came home on leave after his training in Texas. He gave John and me a Tank Destroyer sleeve patch to sew on our jackets. You would see more and more kids in school wearing patches from all branches of the services. It was quite a fad. Jim went to the Pacific to fight, and later he was chosen to go to Corpsman school and became a Hospital Corpsman.

In early 1942 Bud enlisted in the Navy. He also went to Corpsman school after boot camp. He took his boot training at the Great Lakes Naval Training Center, and after Corpsman school went to serve at a Naval Hospital on the East Coast.

France enlisted in the Army in early 1942, and the family once again attended the swearing-in ceremony on the steps of City Hall. France was one of many who were sworn in that day. In basic training all men are given aptitude tests; their test determines what specialty school, if any, the recruit qualifies for. France qualified for OCS (Officers Candidate School) in Brownsville, Texas. It was a 90-day school and, if completed, entitled the graduate to a rank of 2nd Lieu-

Jim — home from Fort Hood, Texas Tank Destroyer School, 1942 *Bud U.S. Navy 1942* *France in Europe 1944*

tenant. They were referred to in the Army as a "90-day wonder" after OCS graduation.

France told the family later how difficult the school was. Every Monday morning, when the cadets would fall in for muster, there would be a few less men in his class. The men who failed the training would be awakened during the middle of the night and told to pack their belongings and they would be shipped out to a new unit or back to their old units. The cadets remaining never saw them again. France said it was hard to sleep on a weekend as this was the time when the failed cadets were aroused from their sleep and sent packing. France graduated from OCS, and Freda and Mom went by train to the graduation ceremonies in Texas. We were all very proud of France for his accomplishment. With only a high school education, he had achieved what many with a college degree could not. After a couple of years of training in the Coast Artillery, he was sent to Europe to take part in the Normandy invasion, June 6, 1944. His outfit was stationed on large floating caissons made from concrete, which were floated from England to just off the shore of Normandy and sunk. On the caisson were mounted anti-aircraft guns which were to protect landing troops from German planes. France remained in Europe and took part in the Battle of the Bulge in the winter of 1944 and 1945. He returned home a hero in our eyes.

I remember, prior to France leaving for Europe, the landlord, Mr. Foster, who rented the house to Sis and Vernard and lived next door, was an engineer for Decoursey Dairy in Leavenworth. He made a large knife for France from a file. It was a very professional job and with the leather scabbard was a first class weapon. I have often wondered what happened to that knife.

Mr. Foster had a workshop in his backyard and was quite an entrepreneur. He had a contract from a company to assemble the components for crystal sets. He hired John and me to work for him one summer. Our job was to wind antenna wire from a large spool of wire into about 20-foot coils that were packed into the box containing the crystal sets. We also sanded the blocks of wood that were used for the base, and there were other tasks necessary to complete the final product. We were paid by the piece. It wasn't much, but was quite a sum for two young kids.

Sis' husband, Vernard Dykes, enlisted in the Army Air Corps, and after his basic training was stationed at Sherman Field, Fort Leavenworth, Kansas, and was a member of the Sherman Air Field Fire Department. During the war it was a busy air field. Our family had a four-star flag in our front window during the war in honor of Bud, France, Jim and Vernard, members of the Armed Forces from the same family.

By the end of 1941, rubber rationing, the first of many wartime rationing regulations, was announced.

With all the young men going into the service and factories gearing up to manufacture war material, jobs in most cities were easier to find. Leavenworth, not being a manufacturing town, was still not benefiting, insofar as good jobs,

*Jim —
home on leave
Me, Titter,
Virginia, John
and Babe
1942*

as were larger cities. A lot of people in Leavenworth were moving to Kansas City or driving daily where jobs were more plentiful. Pop was still working for different farmers in the Kickapoo area. A lot of the sons of farmers were entering the service, which made it easier for Pop to find work, and the pay was getting better as the farmers were getting better prices for their products.

In 1942 the last civilian car built in the United States, a Gray Pontiac, rolled off the production line on February 2nd. Thereafter, automobile plants were used to produce planes, tanks and other war materials.

When the Japanese bombed Pearl Harbor, America was forever changed. The end of the depression came almost overnight. National outrage over Pearl Harbor galvanized the country. Mom and Pop would listen to the news every night, and the news was more meaningful now.

With Bud, France, Jim and Vernard now in the service,

along with many of our cousins and friends, the news took on a new urgency. Rationing would become a way of life. All types of food items, such as sugar, butter, meat and coffee, as well as tires and gasoline, required rationing stamps. No stamps, no rationed items. Lucky Strike cigarettes, which had a green circle on the front of the pack, was changed to an all-white pack. The commercial at the time was, "Lucky Strike green has gone to war." Seems the green paint was needed for war vehicles.

People began planting victory gardens in the front and back yards of their homes. Speed limits were dropped to conserve gasoline. Scrap drives collected paper, metal, cooking oil and tin tooth paste tubes to be used in building war material. In February clocks were turned ahead one hour so there would be more daytime hours for people to work; it was called "war time" (later it would be known as Daylight Savings time), which for most of the country is still in effect. The shortage of silk stockings was a loss to a lot of women, but women simply used eyebrow pencils to draw "seams" on their bare legs. Wartime conservation rules stated shorter hem lengths for women and the number of pockets. Any excess material was eliminated, such as coat cuffs and hoods. All metal fastenings were banned. Men also had restrictions on coat lengths and the width of pant legs.

As men left for war, the women were stepping forward to fill the positions they once held. When the recruiting doors were open to women in 1942, nearly 150,000 would serve in the Women's Army Corps (WAC). The Navy, Marines and Coast Guard would add women units. Women served as military pilots, drivers and mechanics.

Every day brought changes. It is a little ironic that for the 12 years the depression lasted we couldn't afford to buy the things we needed and now, with the war and rationing and with better wages, we still couldn't.

And off to the war went a lot of Hollywood stars. Some who were in the military were: James Stewart, an officer and bomber pilot who flew several missions over Germany; Clark Gable, also in the Army Air Corps as a gunnery instructor, and many more serving in the Navy, Marines and Coast Guard. Women stars entertained troops and headed up war bond drives.

Even school children helped by buying war stamps and bonds. In our school the children would take their dimes and quarters to school and buy war stamps, much like postage stamps. You would paste them in a book, and when the book was full, it would be turned in at the bank for a war bond.

When school was out for the summer in 1942, I joined the Boy Scouts, and one of our civic duties was to help with scrap metal and paper drives. With the help of our scoutmaster or another adult who would drive the truck, we went from house to house collecting newspapers. On other weekends we would go house to house collecting scrap metal. The scout troop went on an overnight campout on the banks of a creek at 18th and Spruce Streets. That area is built up with housing now, and hard to believe it was ever a spot for camping.

The summer passed as other summers had, with work in the garden, cutting wood for the kitchen cook stove and mowing the grass with the old reel mower. We now had a lot more hoeing to do. Pop rented a couple of acres from Ms. Duffey, who lived on 10th Avenue. The two acres would have joined the south side of our pasture but for a one-lane road which divided the two parcels of land. The road led down and around the west side of our land and terminated at the home of the Huffman family.

The Huffmans had five children. One of the boys, Donald, was my age, and he and I, along with John, played together. They also had a daughter, JoAnn, the same age as Babe. They got along so well and remain good friends to this day.

Pop, John, Bill, Babe, Titter and Mary cutting potatoes for spring planting

The garden plot Pop rented was plowed and planted in sweet corn and potatoes. It took a lot of hoeing. Pop bought a couple hundred pounds of seed potatoes in the spring, and they all had to be cut in pieces with a sprout on each piece. Then they had to be planted and covered. It took a long time to plant an acre of potatoes. I was always glad when the job was completed. Now we had to keep the weeds out until fall when the potatoes would be dug and stored in the cellar for use in the winter. It was a lot of work, but we always enjoyed having potatoes all winter long, along with the other vegetables. Pop rented the garden from Ms. Duffey for several years and also rented her pasture land, 10 acres or so. Our cow, Daisy, had a nice heifer calf that spring, and the extra pasture would come in handy during the hot, dry summer when our small pasture wasn't large enough to support more than one cow.

September came and, sure enough, the new school was ready. The new school was named "Howard Wilson." The old Maplewood school was a thing of the past. I was in the sixth grade, John was in the fifth, and Babe was in the first grade; Titter was now in high school. I had a new classmate that year, Richard Simms. The Simms family had moved to Leavenworth from Kansas City, Missouri. Richard's father was transferred in as manager of the Bell Telephone office in Leavenworth. We hit it off from the start and remain good friends today. The new school had a large, grassy playground with all the usual swings, slides, etc. The big playground game at that time was marbles. All the boys would bring their marble bags to school every day, containing peewees, taws, aggies and glassies. One or two of the boys were always a little better at the game than all the rest and usually ended up with "all the marbles."

One afternoon on my way home from school, I spotted Babe sitting on a low wall of stone that fenced in Ms. Duffin's front yard. Ms. Duffin was known by all the kids in the neighborhood as the "goat lady." The goat lady lived alone in a huge two-story house that was set back a good distance from the street. She must have been fairly rich at one time and was probably married, but she now lived alone and had several goats that shared her home. The home was weathered and in need of repair. To get back to Babe, as I approached her, she stood up and wanted to walk home with me. She told me she had played "hooky" that day, and not wanting to get home too early and arouse Mom's suspicion, waited for me. Babe said she had been there all day. She never told me why she didn't want to go to school that particular day. I never told Mom, but I think Babe told her.

We got our first telephone about this time. Pop wasn't too thrilled about adding another expense to the household budget, but Mom and Titter thought we needed it. I don't remember Pop ever making a call on the "new fangle contraption." At that time, operators would answer the phone when you picked up the receiver to make a call by saying, "number please." You would give the operator a four-digit number ,and she would connect you with that number. Bud, France and Jim would call Mom and Pop from time to time

Jim and Clyde Dykes
home on leave
1942

from distant places, and I think Pop finally came to realize that the phone was a pretty good invention after all.

Some of the songs we were listening to on the radio at that time were "The White Cliffs of Dover," "I Left My Heart at the Stage Door Canteen," and "White Christmas." Bing Crosby introduced the song, "White Christmas," in the big movie hit of 1942, *Holiday Inn.* Another movie hit of the year was *Casablanca.* "This is the Army," featuring an all-soldier cast, was touring the country. Irving Berlin would stop the show with his singing of "Oh, How I Hate to Get Up in the Morning."

In November, we heard on the news that the five Sullivan brothers of Iowa were lost when the USS Juneau was sunk in the Pacific. The Armed Forces created the policy that brothers could not serve together on the same ship. This was the greatest patriotic sacrifice by any American family since the Civil War.

The Christmas season in 1942 wasn't the most cheerful time. With so many of the family away in the service, it just wasn't the same, and to make matters worse, Pop had not been paid for work he had done during December. The man for whom he worked promised he would mail Pop his paycheck in plenty of time for Christmas. About a week before Christmas, Pop would come home from working at a different place and ask Mom if his check had arrived that day in the mail. Mom would say, "Not today." This went on until Christmas Eve day. Mom had not done any shopping for the family, as this paycheck was to be our Christmas money. Pop had driven to the post office to check on his money when it had not arrived in the regular mail. The postmaster said it was not there, but there was "one more" load of incoming mail to the post office that day and he was welcome to come back after 4 p.m. and check. Pop returned to the post office at the designated time. We were all in the car holding our breath as Pop went in to the post office. We saw Pop come out with a smile on his lips and an envelope in his hand. The check had arrived. Mom only had a couple of hours to do her shopping before the stores closed. Titter, John, Babe and I were each given a dollar to do our shopping. After stopping by the grocery store for Christmas dinner fixin's, we went home to wrap the gifts and get ready for a Merry Christmas. The check Pop had been waiting for was only about $49, but it was a huge amount to us. To this date, I tear up when I think back to that Christmas of 1942 and how close it was that Mom and Pop would not be able to provide a Christmas for the family.

The new year, 1943, brought more shortages and ration restrictions. Butter, cheese, flour, fish and canned goods joined the list of rationed items. The red and blue ration stamps became a way of life. Shoes were rationed to three pairs a year, and the rubber shortage curtailed the manufacturing of new sneakers. The gas shortage limited driving to work and back with little left over for pleasure driving.

Pop found it necessary to find work close to home, as the

shortage of fuel made it impossible to drive the long distance to work around the Kickapoo area. He was lucky and found a job at the packing house in Leavenworth. It was a hard job, but the pay was good and it was inside work with regular hours. His job was in the "tankage" room. This was a large room with a huge steam cooking vat where all the discarded parts of the animals were hauled by cart, dumped into the steam vat and cooked, resulting in a product that was used for hog feed. The hides of the cattle were sent to a large room in the basement where they were "salted" with rock salt and stacked and allowed to dry.

Mom would watch for the mailman every day, hoping to get a letter from "the boys." They were very good about writing and did so whenever they had the opportunity, although they were not able to write much about their movements or anything that could be considered as military secrets. When they would write from overseas, their letters were heavily censored and key words or phrases would be cut out. Jim was now in the Pacific war zone, and Frank and France were still in the United States. Frank's wife, Ruth, was living with her parents. Freda, France's wife, was living in a rented house on North 4th Street. Vernard and Sis were living in a "Mr. Foster" apartment, as Vernard was now stationed at Sherman Field at Fort Leavenworth.

Summer would bring an end to grade school for me. I would be attending junior high come fall. That summer went as the previous summer, garden and yard work, milking the cow, feeding chickens and keeping firewood cut for the kitchen cook stove. The summer was not all work. John and I would play with other boys our age. Baseball and "war games" were favored games. We would also walk to the library every week or so and bring home several books to read. The "Hardy Boys" was always a special one, and we were chewed out by Mom, and later in the evening when Pop got home, because we were so engrossed in a Hardy Boys mystery that we sometimes neglected our hoeing or grass-cutting duties.

An old widow lady who lived on 10th Avenue in a large brick home (her large back yard backed up to the street in front of our house) called me over to her house one day and asked if I wanted to earn some money. I told her, "Sure," and she wanted me to clean up the yard and shrubs around her house and pile it in one spot for burning. I went to work, pulled weeds, cut grass, trimmed the bushes around the house and stacked all in a neat pile. I worked for two or three hours, then knocked on her door and told her I was finished. She came out, looked around and said it looked fine. She went in the house after telling me to wait, then, came out with 50 cents. I was excited at having so much money and told her if she needed me for any more work I was available.

About two weeks later, the old lady called me over and asked if I would clean out her basement, clean up, sweep, knock down the cobwebs and stack everything. I said sure, remembering the 50 cents for doing a lot less work. I went to work and really put my heart and soul into that job. I worked the better part of that day, doing a first-class cleanup on that dark, dusty, old basement. I finished the work with webs in my hair and coal dust all over me. She came down to the basement and said it looked great. I was excited about the prospects of a huge payday because, after all, I worked twice as hard in the basement as I had on the yard job. She handed me a quarter and thanked me. I went home disappointed and felt like I had been taken. I learned that day a great lesson that life isn't always fair. Sucker me once, shame on you. Sucker me twice, shame on me.

We would walk to town on Saturdays to see a movie when we could come up with the 15 cents admission price at that time. The movies were war-oriented. *Heaven Can Wait* with Gene Tierney and Don Ameche; *Lassie Come Home*, starring

83

Bud — home on leave from Navy, with Bill; John on "Old Tom" with Bobbie and Judy. Circa 1943.

Roddy McDowell, and *This is the Army,* which had been made into a motion picture. Charlie Chan and Sherlock Holmes were now fighting the Germans and Japanese spies. The newsreels gave us graphic scenes of the battlefield in Europe and Pacific Islands. All the films had trailers urging us to buy war bonds. On Broadway, the musical, *"Oklahoma,"* opened.

The summer of 1943 passed and it was time to start school. Junior high would be a new experience, a different room for each class. John was in the sixth grade and Babe in the second grade at Howard Wilson. Titter was now a sophomore in high school.

I walked to school, which was quite a distance from home. I walked by Richard Simms house and we walked together, along with Raymond Kohler and Kenneth Powell, who lived in Richard's neighborhood. We were all beginning junior high experiences together. We became good friends and remain so to this day, although Kenneth Powell died a few years ago.

Some afternoons after school we would walk to town and then home, which wasn't too far out of the way. On one of these detours to home we passed a small bakery on 5th

Street, across from the library, and I noticed a sign in the window, "Help Wanted." I went in, and the baker-owner hired me after school to clean and wash pots and pans that had been used to bake all the goodies that day. It sounded like the kind of job I could get my teeth into. It paid 15 cents an hour, with no benefits except an occasional overbaked cinnamon roll, which were "accidents." Getting the burnt sugar out of those pans was hard work and required using a big putty knife, then soaking and scrubbing until the pan was clean. It was a very boring job and it didn't last long. I could not see a future in that field of work.

Pop's job and steady paychecks allowed us to run city water to the house, and also to hook onto the city sewer line. This meant a bathroom with a bathtub. No more long trips to the outhouse through deep snow or baths in a tub located in the wash room behind the kitchen. I think it was about this time that we also had natural gas piped into the house, which meant hot water and a new gas cook stove for Mom. We still heated the house with wood.

The fall of that year Ray Kohler took on a paper route, the morning *Kansas City Star,* and wanted me to share the route with him. I accepted the offer and we started the route. The papers were dropped off close to the starting point of our route. We would have to fold the papers in such a way as to allow throwing the paper to the front porch of the customers. It was a long route, but no more papers than the other routes. Our route was on the southwest edge of Leavenworth, and the houses were far apart. Having the route meant I had to get up at 5 a.m., get dressed and walk to Ray's house. He would be ready to go, and usually his mother would have something ready for us to eat, cereal or a sweet roll, which was good. We would proceed to our "route" and start folding. With all the papers in our huge canvas bags, and each taking a side of the street, we would start throwing the *Kansas City Star.*

The paper route during the fall was nice, easy work except for the early hour. We had certain houses we hurried by because of a big dog or two, but the job was rather enjoyable. Then came winter. The route was a lot harder, and sometimes the $15 we each made for a month's work didn't seem that much. Like at 5 a.m., on a cold January morning when the snow would crunch with each step, and your breath would fog the cold air around you. It was harder and harder to get out of a warm bed into a cold bedroom when you could see your breath, put on cold clothes and shoes and leave a cold house into a colder outdoors. I was awake by 5:00 a.m., but sometimes Mom would have to come into our bedroom and talk me out of bed. I was always glad after getting dressed and heading out the door that I had succeeded one more time in beating the urge to quit such a God-awful job. I did save enough money to buy a bicycle in the spring of 1944. Ray Kohler and I gave up the route when school was out in the spring.

In the summer of 1944 I turned 14, and Pop was able to land a summer job for me at the packing house where he worked. It was a union shop, but I was not required to join the union because of my age. I was required to get a Social Security number. I applied for and got my Social Security card with my nickname, Bill Williams, and not my legal name, William. I never used William at that time, but did so in later years.

My job at the packing house was to push a "gut wagon." This was a two-wheeled cart with a metal box shaped much like a wheelbarrow tray. As the butcher on the "killing floor" would cut a cow, hanging by its hind legs, open down the belly, I would push the "gut cart" under the neck of the cow and catch everything that wasn't to be kept; intestines, unborn baby calves, etc. The Government meat inspector would, at that time, check the liver. If the liver looked okay, he would

86

stamp the beef with an inked stamp, and the beef would be pushed along the overhead rail to the next operation. I would push the two-wheel cart, loaded with the inside of the cow, to the tankage room, and it was dumped, much like dumping cement from a wheelbarrow, into the top of a huge metal tank, with the bottom of the tank extending into the basement. This is the area where Pop worked. The metal tank was a huge steam cooker, as previously described. There were two of us pushing gut wagons, and it kept us busy trying to keep up with the butchers on the killing floor.

When the last cart load had been pushed to the tankage room for the day, we would start cleaning the killing room floor. The butchers would be through for the day, as their job was finished, and would leave work. A few of us "non-butchers" would stay until the killing floor was spotless. Heavy steam hoses were used to clean all the equipment and floors. For this job, I was paid 60 cents an hour. It doesn't seem like much today, but at that time I had more money on payday than I'd ever had before.

One morning when I arrived at work, my boss asked me if I would like a new job. I said yes. I knew any new job would be better than the one I had. He said I would work at the scale weighing the beef halves, tagging them with the weight and pushing them along the overhead rail to the man who put the white cheesecloth shroud over the entire half of beef prior to the beef being pushed into the huge meat cooler. I enjoyed this job, but still had to stay and help clean up.

I was able to give Mom some of my wages and also buy new clothes for John and me for the coming school year. John was left with the garden and yard work, so I never minded sharing my wages with him. Pushing a gut wagon was not a very romantic job description, so I never used it on any future job applications when listing my prior work experience. I would just put down "packing house."

There were some exciting days at work in the packing house, like the time we got in a carload of Brahmas from Texas. It was almost impossible to keep them in the cattle pens with their jumping ability. Some of these Brahmas successfully jumped the fence and escaped into the downtown area, where they wrecked havoc on several cars and yard fences. The Police were notified, and after several hours all the cattle were rounded up and returned to the packing house or shot before they totally destroyed the City of Leavenworth. It was fun watching the men who worked the cattle pens on days when we received a shipment of Brahmas.

The union at the packing house had been talking about going out on strike for better wages, as their contract was ending. The union was made up of meat cutters, so Pop's job was non-union, and I was too young to join the union. When they did strike, it did not interfere with our jobs, except after a few days into the strike, Pop did not have material for making tankage. He stayed home for a time until the strike ended. I, not a union member, was able to work every day doing odd jobs, such as cleaning equipment, etc.

One Sunday morning, after the strike was ended, Pop went to work. He went in and emptied the huge cooker that made the tankage so as to have it ready for Monday morning. Mom received a phone call from the hospital telling her that Pop had been brought in after losing a large and dangerous amount of blood from a cut on his leg. It seems that when Pop had walked into the packing house that morning and proceeded to his work site, he started to bleed from a cut on his leg and left a trail of blood to some point in the packing house where he collapsed unconscious. Luckily for Pop, another Sunday worker reported to work shortly after Pop and spotted the trail of blood, following it to where Pop lay unconscious. He was able to stop some of the bleeding with a cloth tied around the wound and called for an ambulance. Pop was rushed to the hospital and given blood. He had been near death from the blood loss.

The doctor examined the wound and extracted a small sliver of steel which had worked its way to an artery and punctured it. Seems that a few years before this incident, while cutting wood, Pop was using a wedge to split some wood and a tiny sliver of the steel wedge had been knocked off the wedge from the sledge hammer blows and had ended up in the leg. Pop thought he had only suffered a small cut and thought no more about it until it had worked its way to the artery. He was home a few days recuperating and then back to work. Very lucky for all of us.

One Sunday in late fall Pop loaded Mom, John, Babe and me into the car and we drove to Kickapoo. We parked at the Truman Gwartney farm and waited while Pop hitched up a team of mules to an old "spring wagon." It had a spring seat in front and a large grain box. Truman had loaned the team and wagon to Pop for the day so that we could gather black walnuts from trees in a large wooded area that bordered the Missouri River and Missouri Pacific Railroad tracks. It was a few miles from Kickapoo and took us two or three hours to reach the spot. We found the ground surrounding the walnut trees covered with black walnuts. We began gathering the nuts, which still had the hulls on them, and filled the gunny sacks we had brought with us. Sometime during the gathering, we stopped and ate the picnic lunch Mom had prepared. It was a nice fall day, and we all had a fun time. About 4:00 p.m. we had filled all the gunny sacks, so we headed back to Kickapoo with our load of nuts.

We were on a road that paralleled the Missouri Pacific Railroad tracks, a road which was used only by farmers in the area and was little traveled. Pop knew of the walnut trees from having cut wood in the area from years past.

Pop was whipping up the team of mules pretty good. We

kids were bouncing up and down on the many sacks of nuts. Mom was sitting on the spring seat with Pop and holding on with both hands. Mom asked Pop why he was driving so fast, and we heard Pop tell Mom that there was a freight train due to pass us about 5:00 p.m. and he was trying to reach the turnoff road before the train came by. Pop knew the team of mules fairly well, having worked for Truman before and used the team of mules on jobs. Pop said the mules were very "skittish" and the train would probably scare them into trying to get away from the train and could overturn the wagon. This frightened Mom and the rest of us. Our fears heightened even more as off in the distance behind us we heard the faint sound of a train whistle. We had about a quarter of a mile to go before reaching the road which would lead us away from the river and the train tracks. Pop was standing up now urging the team of mules on as fast as they could run. We were all holding on for dear life. We could now see the road ahead where we would turn. We could also hear the train coming, and by looking back could also see the headlights on the big steam engine as the road was straight and you could see a long distance in both directions. The train was gaining on us, and we could just see the mules going out of control and running wild with the wagon being overturned and throwing us into the path of the freight train. The team of mules were now running all out ,and we reached the junction and turned off with the wheels of the wagon sliding in the sharp turn. We had made it! With the mules now headed away from the passing freight train, Pop pulled the team to a stop, allowing them to get their wind and the freight train to rush by on its way to who knows where. We were all very relieved and finished our outing of nut gathering. Pop returned the team of mules and we headed home.

Everything evolved around the war in 1944. The Allied forces were winning, and the nation was shocked by details

France with his buddies — 1944 in France

of the mass murders of citizens by the German military at Birkenau and Auschwitz. Germany introduced the pilotless "robot" bomb and the highly destructive V-2, a supersonic rocket, doing terrible damage to British cities.

Salvage drives were still in full swing, and nearly half the country's needs in steel, tin, and paper were provided by civilian salvage efforts.

On the radio in 1944, we were listening to Jack Benny, Fibber McGee and Molly, and Bob Hope. "I'll Be Seeing You" topped the charts as song of the year. It was written in 1939, but became popular because the lyrics seemed to capture the mood of couples separated by the war. We learned of the plane crash that took the life of the "big band" leader Glen Miller. Major Glen Miller was director of the Army Air Corps band and was on a flight from London to Paris at the time of the crash.

On June 6th, 1944, D-Day, the winning back of Europe began with the Normandy Invasion, "The Longest Day," with General Eisenhower as the Supreme Commander. We had no idea that our brother, France, was part of the invasion forces. The invasion was top secret, and Operation Overlord was a surprise to Americans.

There had been talk on the radio that something big was in the works, but no one knew what or when. The war was something we were learning to live with, long lines at the half-empty meat counter, and trying to keep track of all those rationing stamps. People were heard saying, "I wish this war would end," as if saying it would somehow make it so.

Richard Simms, Ray Kohler, Kenneth Powell and I would walk to school every day. We were all in the eighth grade. Kenneth Powell had six brothers; one was a little older than Kenneth and was too young to go in the service, but the other five brothers were in the service. A flag hung in their front room window with five blue stars on it. One morning we walked by his house, and one of the blue stars had been replaced with a gold star. Kenneth had lost a brother to the war. Seems like everyone in our class and school had brothers and sisters in the service. A girl in my class, last name Shockley, had a brother in the battle for Iwo Jima who was present for the flag raising, although I don't think he was one of the group photographed.

Sometimes after school we would walk home through town and stop in the bowling alley on Cherokee Street. Once in a while the manager of the alley would want us to set pins. We had to set the pins by hand as this was before the pin setting racks came into being. Seems as though we would earn 15 cents a line and sometimes would receive a small tip. We would only set pins for an hour or so because we would have to get home — chores to do.

School was out at the end of May, and I was looking forward to a summer of fun, swimming at the "Wolman Park" pool and playing baseball, but again Pop came to the rescue and saved me from all those foolish notions of a "fun summer."

He had hauled wheat to the local grain elevator for several years for a number of wheat farmers in the area and had become acquainted over the years with a Mr. Reid (pronounced "Red"), who managed the local grain elevator. Pop had just recently met Mr. Reid in a store in Leavenworth, and Pop learned that they were going to need another worker at the elevator in a few days to work during the wheat harvest. Pop volunteered me for the job. Mr. Reid wanted me to come to the elevator so he could look me over and to see if I could handle the job, as I would only be 15 in May.

Pop took me to the elevator one evening before dark, and I met Mr. Reid who gave us a tour of the elevator and explained that I would be working at the very top of the elevator. He proceeded to take us to the top to show me my work area. Mr. Reid walked over to a switch and flipped it on. A huge belt, which ran to the top of the elevator, began to turn, and I noticed "hand holds" and "foot steps" on the belt. I later learned this was called a "man lift." As the hand hold and foot step came by and started up toward the top of the elevator, Mr. Reid grabbed the hand hold and stepped onto the foot step and began ascending, calling for us to follow suit. Pop had no fear of height, having worked on the high-rise buildings in Kansas City, grabbed the hand hold and stepped onto the foot step and started up. Now, it was my turn. I have never been too brave when it came to heights. I think this came from Mom who told me a story when I was very young about a neighbor boy who wanted to play football at school, but his mother said, "No," as he might get hurt. The young neighbor boy was mad at his mother and went out to play. He climbed a tall tree, fell and broke his arm and leg and was laid up for several weeks. I don't know if this played a part in my fear of heights, or if I used this story to cover my fear.

I reached out and grabbed the hand hold and stepped onto the foot step and began the long ride up the side of the elevator to the top. I didn't dare look down. I kept looking up and saw Mr. Reid finally step off to his left onto the floor, and let loose of the hand hold. Pop followed suit, and now it was my turn to try and get off this thing. I stepped off and let go of the hand hold, and there I was at the very top of this grain elevator, which was nearly a hundred feet tall.

Mr. Reid began showing me my job. There were small railroad tracks running the length and between the six or eight huge concrete silos that held the wheat. On these tracks was a "car" that ran up and down the length of the elevator. It was propelled by a wide "V" shaped belt which ran around some rollers on the car and, by pulling a large lever, would cause the rollers to tighten against the fast-moving belt, causing the car to move forward or backward, depending on which way the lever was moved. The huge belt ran in a continuous circle from the one end of the elevator through the rollers on the car to the far end of the elevator and back to the other end. The wheat was carried from the pit where wheat trucks dumped their load to the top of the elevator where it was dumped onto the belt running the length of the elevator. My job would be to listen for the phone call which would tell me to move the rail car to a specific "tank." Even numbers to the right and odd numbers to the left. Another lever on the car would trip the grain to the right or to the left. The grain was dumped into different tanks according to the moisture content of the wheat. As a grain truck was directed into the elevator, and prior to the actual dumping of the grain, a sample was taken and tested for moisture content. The load was weighed and a phone call to the top of the elevator was made directing me to dump the load in a specific tank. I would run the dump car to the correct tank and direct the discharge chute, either right or left depending on which tank the wheat was to be dumped. As long as the trucks were dumping wheat with approximately the same moisture content, there was no need to move the car.

I listened to all the instructions and gave the right answers, I guess, because I was hired. But all the time I was listening to my instructions, I kept thinking about getting on that man lift for the long ride down, hanging onto that big belt.

The following Monday I reported to work at 7 a.m. I was introduced to the rest of the crew. There were four of us, plus Mr. Reid. Mr. Reid worked the desk, getting wheat samples for testing, weighing the trucks prior to unloading and after the load was dumped. The others would work getting the trucks in and operating the lift which raised the truck for dumping. Mr. Reid would be the one who would call me by phone instructing me, at the top, where to dump the wheat. But the wheat harvest had not started and, in fact, we had a fairly wet, early summer and the harvest had been delayed somewhat because of the wet conditions. So, for now, our job was to clean up around the elevator, such as cutting grass and chopping weeds along the railroad tracks which ran close to the elevator. In general, just getting ready for the coming harvest. We had about two weeks of this type of work, but by the end of the second week, some farmers south of Leavenworth were beginning to combine some wheat and haul it to the elevator. The gradual start of the harvest gave us time to work the kinks out, so by the time the harvest was in full swing we were ready.

By now I was having no fear of the man lift and had learned to maneuver the "dump car" and get it into the right position for dumping the wheat into the proper tank. Each day we were beginning to see more farmers hauling their wheat to the elevator. Then we had a wet, rainy weekend and all combining stopped, but by the first of the week, the weather turned sunny and the harvest started in earnest. At first, we were finishing the day at about 6:00 p.m., but within a few days every farmer wanted to get his wheat in while the weather was nice, and a long line of wheat trucks were still to be unloaded after dark. This meant we were working until midnight just to get all the trucks unloaded. We would finish around midnight and would be back to work at 6:00 a.m.

One night I was at my post working the dump car when Mr. Reid called on the phone and said he was sending one of the other workers up to relieve me. He wanted me and another guy to go home and get some sleep, then come back and relieve the other two. So, at midnight I took off for home to get a few hours of sleep. As Pop and I were driving up the street, we could see the grain trucks lined up for four full blocks, waiting to get their grain unloaded.

I was back to work before 6 a.m. the following morning. The two who had stayed on the night before took off to get a few hours rest. The farmers pitched in and helped with the unloading of their grain. Luckily this was the only night that we unloaded grain for 24 hours straight. The wheat harvest was on a downward curve, and our work hours were more civilized, although there was still much of the wheat harvest remaining.

A week or so later the harvest ended and we began the task of loading grain cars. We would move a grain car, which was on a siding, by using a large crow bar type tool and inserting it under the wheel of a grain car and slowly roll it into position for loading. A large grain chute was used to move the wheat from the storage silo to the grain car. When the car was loaded, it was moved up the siding by means previously described. When several cars had been loaded, the railroad was notified; they would back a locomotive onto the siding and haul the wheat to market, or wherever they take wheat. They didn't tell *me*.

My job with the grain elevator came to an end after about a week of cleanup around the elevator. I really enjoyed the experience and had made more money that summer than I'd ever made before.

CHAPTER 6

The War and Rationing Comes to an End

WHEN PRESIDENT TRUMAN approved the order to drop the atomic bomb on Japan in 1945, the world would be changed forever.

While Bud, France, Jim and Vernard did not immediately come home from the service, we knew they had survived the war and we looked forward to their return, along with all of our cousins and friends.

The war's end brought an end to rationing. With few goods available to buy during the war and with good wages, large nest eggs had accumulated and people wanted to buy things and spend money, causing

Jim in Japan
1945

97

countless shortages. Stores were full of new wonders, including frozen orange juice, ballpoint pens, aerosol spray insecticides, butane cigarette lighters and Tupperware. Auto factories began to build cars once again. Long lists of names of eager buyers were posted on the walls of auto dealers' showrooms, waiting their turn to grab up one of the new 1946 models as soon as they arrived at the dealer's lot. It was suspected that "under the table" deals were made to get your name moved higher on the "list." Some of the automobile makers at that time, who are no longer around, were: Hudson, Nash, Studebaker, Packard and later came the Tucker and Kaiser and Frazier, named for and built by the Liberty ship builders during the war.

In 1945 Pop and Mom saved enough money to purchase a 160-acre farm in Kickapoo, something that they had wanted ever since losing their farm to the bank after World War I. Pop was still working at the packing house, and since Mom did not want to move back to the country, farming was done on a limited basis. Weekends were spent at the new farm working it part-time. The farm had been purchased from the Spencer family, who had lived and farmed it for many years. The farm was forever known as the "old Spencer place." It had a fairly nice old two-story farm house and several large barns on it. It also had a eight or ten-cow dairy milking barn. Half of the land was farm land, the other half woods and pasture.

Pop attended a farm sale shortly after purchasing the farm and bought a team of horses with harness, several pieces of horse-drawn farm equipment, a single 16-inch sulkey plow, a corn planter, a dump rake, along with harrow and two-row cultivator. He also bought a large farm wagon for hauling hay which could be converted to a grain wagon, and a two-horse buggy. Most farmers were going to tractors, so Pop was able to buy the horse-drawn equipment at a very reasonable price. The rest of 1945 was spent getting the farm cleaned up and putting up hay. The farm came with a fairly large patch of alfalfa hay, which was mowed, raked and pitched onto the hay wagon and hauled to the barn where it was put into the loft of the large main barn, which had horse stables and a large grain bin on the ground level, and a basement level which acted as a loafing area for cattle. The barn had been built on the side of a hill which gave it the three levels. Pop bought the rope and large fork used for unloading the hay from the wagon, and by using a team of horses on the opposite end of the barn, would pull the hay up to the loft door. It was then carried by a track running the length of the barn and deposited by pulling a "trip rope" which allowed the hay to be dropped into the loft. The large fork was retrieved back to the wagon by pulling on the trip rope and backing the horses to the starting point. The large fork was driven into the pile of hay on the wagon; the fork had teeth which were set into the hay, and a yell to the other end of the barn where the driver of the team of horses would again raise the huge wad of hay up and into the barn. It took the three of us to unload the hay. Pop would be on the wagon setting the two-prong fork, I, on the other end of the barn driving the team of horses, and John, in the loft directing the placement of the hay.

Pop had an old Chevy pickup, and after many hours of driving with Pop as the instructor, John and I were allowed to drive the truck to the farm in Kickapoo through the week (Pop was working at the packing house) and cut the hay, rake it the following day and be ready for the weekend when it was hauled to the barn. The hay was cut three or four times a summer, and it seemed we were hauling hay all the time.

Before allowing John or me to drive the truck, Pop had a checklist of do's and don'ts we had to abide by. Don't speed, keep far to the right when approaching the top of a hill on the narrow two-lane gravel road, as you never knew what was coming up the other side of the hill. Always check the oil and water, and **never, never** leave the emergency brake on when driving.

One morning John and I headed out to the farm, which was about 15 miles from our home in Leavenworth, about five miles past the town of Kickapoo. John and I arrived at the farm and, getting out of the truck, smelled something burning. A fear came over us as we discovered I had failed to release the emergency brake. We never told Pop, but he probably knew when, after that incident, the old truck would never hold itself on a hill when parked with the emergency brake on.

That fall I was a freshman at the junior high school "top dog." Donald Huffman, who lived behind us about a block, was working at Callahan's drug store, delivering prescriptions and working behind the soda fountain. He told me that Mike Gnip, the owner who had bought the drug store from Mr. Callahan and kept the name, was looking for another "jerk" and delivery boy. I figured I could handle the "jerk" part, and since I had my own bicycle, could probably handle the delivery part as well. I went in and talked to Mr. Gnip and was hired. I liked Mr. Gnip from the start, as he always treated us well and was easy for a 15-year-old to talk to. Mike, as everyone called him, worked from early a.m. to late at night. He was a pharmacist, and the prescription counter was at the very back of the long, narrow drug store. He worked filling prescriptions behind a high counter with a large open window, which gave him a good view of the whole drug store. We would close at 10 p.m., and sometimes Richard Simms, Ray Kohler and Kenneth Powell would meet me and we would walk downtown doing nothing in particular. We would walk back by the drug store around 11 p.m. and could see Mike Gnip still behind the prescription counter working.

Mr. Callahan, the former owner of the drug store, had a son who continued working at the drug store after Mike bought it. I have forgotten his first name, but he broke me in behind the soda fountain. He showed me the art of making banana splits, milk shakes, sodas, fountain cokes and the famous Callahan root beer and root beer floats. We used an old ice shaver to make all our fountain drinks. It made them all special. There were two or three small tables in the front of the store adjacent to the soda fountain, and during the evening they were always full. The large fountain root beer sold for a nickel, and the float was 10 cents. Mr. Callahan's son ran the drug store as far as ordering stock and checking out customers who would purchase drug store items. Donald Huffman and I were to work the soda fountain and deliver prescriptions. Donald and I would alternate nights delivering prescriptions. We would both work the fountain, and the one who had the job of delivering prescriptions would hop on the bike, with the prescription in a small bag over his shoulder, and take off. Early in the evening, while it was still light, it wasn't bad, but after dark it was hard to find the right house. And with dogs chasing you and the dogs inside the fenced yards where you were making your delivery, Don and I were always glad when it was the other one's responsibility to make the delivery. We would have to collect for the prescription, and Mike would always give us the correct change for the customer. I really enjoyed my job at Callahan's Drug Store.

One evening in late November while working behind the fountain, I noticed the large door of the fire station, which was just across the street, go up, and one of the fire trucks pulled out making a left turn and stopped two houses up from the drug store. The few people who were in the drug store at that time, including Mike Gnip and myself, walked out the front door to observe the action, as it was so close to the drug store. The firemen were running back and forth from the house to their truck, hauling in boxes of equipment. At about this time, an ambulance arrived. After several minutes, the ambulance attendants carried a blanket-covered stretcher out of the house, slid it into their vehicle and departed. We observed all the action but didn't know what had happened until later. A couple of firemen came over to the drug store, which wasn't uncommon, to get a coke and told us the story. It seems a young man was taking a bath when he accidentally pulled a small electric heater into the bathtub with him and was electrocuted. I knew who lived in the house, but was shocked to learn that the "young man" they spoke of was one of my classmates, Earl Jones. He was just 16 years of age.

One Friday night in early spring Pop said he wished he had one of our horses at the house so that he could plow the garden. The two horses we had were pastured for the winter at a farm not far from our farm in Kickapoo. The Spencer farm we had bought needed work done on the pasture fences, so Pop had made arrangements with a neighbor to keep our horses during the winter. The winter pasture had running water and plenty of grass.

I volunteered to walk to Kickapoo the next day, being Saturday, and ride one of the horses into Leavenworth. It was about 15 miles to where the horses were pastured. After breakfast the following morning, I set out walking. It was a long walk, but we walked just about everywhere we went. We walked to school, we walked to town, we walked to our friends' house, so walking was not just something we did for exercise once or twice a week. I arrived at the pasture where the horses were kept about noon. I had stopped by our farm and picked up a bridle and rope. It took some time to locate the horses because the pasture was quite large, with hills and ravines, and also contained a lot of timber.

After spotting the two horses, Tom and Dan, I approached them with the rope hidden behind me, hoping they would allow me to walk up and slip the rope around their necks. Boy, was I mistaken. After a full winter of running free, they were not about to surrender to my advances. They took off running, kicking up their heels at me, as if to say we're not about to get caught and put to work like last spring.

I chased them for hours all over that pasture. It was getting late in the afternoon before I finally got a rope around Tom's neck and slipped the bridle on.

We started back to Leavenworth, and I could see that it would be dark before we reached the highway taking us into Leavenworth, and I sure didn't want to be riding a horse after dark along a busy highway. We got into the town of Kickapoo just as the sun was setting, and I had come up with a plan. I would ask Kitty Atkinson if I could leave old Tom tied up in her back yard until morning. She said I could, and we left a bucket of water for Tom, and I started walking to Leavenworth — and *home*.

I arrived home about 8:00 or 9:00 p.m., and Mom had been worried about me. She had saved supper for me, and I fell asleep while eating. I have never been as tired as I was that night. If it had been **just** the walk out to Kickapoo and riding old Tom back to Leavenworth, it wouldn't have been bad. It was chasing the horses for two or three hours that took its toll.

Sunday morning Pop drove John and me out to Kitty's house. We got old Tom, and John and I took turns riding back to Leavenworth. Pop got the garden plowed Sunday afternoon, and everything turned out okay.

Kitty Atkinson lived in a small house in Kickapoo and ran the telephone switchboard for the Kickapoo area in her living room. Pop would do work for Kitty from time to time, plowing the garden or other work. John and I would sometimes go with him and got to know her fairly well. She was a small lady who had broken her back as a small child and carried the results with her, as she was stooped over with a large lump on her back. She was the nicest person and always treated us with kindness.

By the fall of 1945, Bud, France, Jim and Vernard had all been discharged from the service, along with our cousins and friends, and were now home and working. Bud went back to work for the Federal Prison in Leavenworth; France went to work at the Command and General Staff College at Fort Leavenworth, and Jim took his test at the Federal Prison and was hired. He later applied for the position of Medical Technical Assistant (MTA) and got the job. His training as a medic in the Army and his experience in working at Mehl and Schott's Drug Store came in handy.

Vernard remained at the Sherman Field Fire Dept. as a civilian. It was a relief with the war over and having everyone home again. Many families were not as fortunate as ours; their sons and daughters paid the ultimate price and would not be returning home.

In the spring of 1946 John and I were working on the farm in Kickapoo; just about every weekend and when school was out, we went to the farm full-time. Pop bought five or six milk cows; they required milking morning and night. Pop was still working at the packing house, so that left John and me to work the farm.

It was a long and lonely summer at the Kickapoo farm. We had no electricity, only oil lamps for light and a battery radio to listen to and no telephone. We would start the day milking and add the milk to the night-before milk, which had been kept in a milk cooler, hauling it about a mile to the main road in the buggy, so as to be there by 8:00 a.m. It was picked up by the Co-op milk truck, and milk cans from the previous day would be left. We would take the empty milk cans back to the farm and fix something to eat. After breakfast, we would start plowing or cutting hay.

As we took our milk down the lane to the pick-up point by the Co-op milk truck, we passed the Rasdales' farm. The Rasdales family consisted of two brothers and their sister. They were in their sixties, I guess, and farmed the 80 or so acres that their parents had left when they passed on. All work on the farm was done by horses, and on Saturdays the three of them could be seen driving their wagon into Leavenworth to do their shopping. They would leave early Saturday morning and arrive in town before noon and leave their team and wagon at Hay Market Square while shopping.

In their barn and up on blocks was a 1919 Dodge touring car. They apparently drove the car for only one year, as the license plate on the car was for the year 1919. They, as a lot of "old timers," never trusted the new-fangled contraption and felt more secure behind a team of trusted horses.

Pop and Mom would come out to the farm on weekends, and things seemed to get back to normal. Mom would cook some great meals on the old wood cook stove while Pop, John and I would plow, plant corn or put up hay.

Through the winter Pop had made weekly visits to the local livestock sale barn and had purchased a good number of cows and calves. We now had 20 or 30 head of cattle and five or six horses. That spring Pop took on the job of feeding out about a hundred head of hogs for the packing house. It was a busy summer, and we didn't get to town very much.

We were sure glad when fall came and we started back to school. Pop sold the milk cows, as there was no way he would be able to continue working at the packing house and get the milking done. That fall we continued to work on the farm every weekend until we had the hay put up and 30 or 40 acres of corn harvested. The hogs had been fattened and returned to the packing house. The corn was all harvested by hand. The team of horses would pull the wagon down the

105

rows of corn; Pop would be on one side of the wagon, shucking out two rows; John and I would each take a row on the other side of the wagon. In all, we would shuck out four rows each trip through the field.

When the wagon was full, we would haul it to one end of the milk barn where it was unloaded and stored. Then back to the corn fields. We used a "shucking peg," which was a knife-like tool with leather finger loops which fit over the four fingers of your right hand. The tool was used to grab the corn shuck and pull it from the ear of corn. The ear of corn was then snapped from the corn stalk and thrown into the wagon. On the wagon was a "bump board" which stuck up above the sideboards of the wagon and made it possible to throw the ear of corn into the wagon without throwing it over the wagon. The last of the corn was harvested late in the fall, and we were all glad when the last ear hit the bump board. Pop sold most of the corn to a large feed lot which was south and west of Kickapoo. We kept enough corn for our own livestock. We spent several weekends loading out the corn into a grain truck and hauling it to the feed lot.

I was now in the 10th grade at Leavenworth High School and enjoyed school. It seemed easy after a long summer of farming.

France took command of the Army Reserve Unit, 'B' Battery of the 758th Field Artillery Battalion, at Fort Leavenworth in 1947. The Unit had approximately 30 members. France made Captain when he became commanding officer of the unit. I joined the Reserve Unit in the fall of 1947 and began attending weekly drills at Fort Leavenworth. We trained with the 105 Howitzer as well as other Army equipment. We had close order drills and, for the most part, it was like basic training.

I also signed up for high school Army ROTC and had more training in drilling. There was classroom work, as well as rifle training. There was a firing range in the basement of the ROTC building, which was about a block from the high school. We trained with the "old" 1903 Bolt Action, 30 caliber rifle, which had been the mainstay of the military since before the 1st World War and was still being used by the military at the beginning of the 2nd World War. It was replaced with

the M1 and Carbine shortly after the start of WWII. I made Corporal during my sophomore year and was named squad leader.

A classmate, Maris Brady, worked at Jahn's Supermarket. In conversation one day, he told me that there was an opening for a stock boy at the market. I went to the market after school and applied for the job and was hired. Two brothers, Arthur and Howard Jahn, had taken over the supermarket when their father had retired from the business. Art, as Arthur was known, had charge of the grocery part of the store, and Howard headed up the produce department, which included the meat and dairy sections.

I really enjoyed the grocery business and was anxious to get to work after school and on Saturdays. The store was closed on Sundays. Art and Howard would argue with each other over the smallest details. I would report for work at about 3:30 p.m., shortly after school was out, and if Howard was not there at the time, Art would put me to work stocking shelves in the grocery department. When Howard returned to the store, he would "jump" Art about stealing me from the produce department. They would become quite loud, and I felt as if I was put in the middle of an ongoing family feud. Howard would usually win, and he would have me for the rest of the day in the produce department, sacking potatoes into 10-pound bags, trimming lettuce, celery or other vegetables before placing them on the display counters for sale. I believe I was hired to work in the produce department as Maris Brady worked in the grocery department for Art, but Art would steal me away from Howard every chance he got.

But for all the squabbling between the two, they treated me well, and I guess both of them wanting me to work for them spoke well of my work.

One day, after reporting for work in the late spring, Howard asked me if I would like to go up north with him. I was speechless for a few moments, and in my mind I thought of Canada, Alaska, the great Northwest territory, and I could hardly control my excitement as a loud "yes" poured from my trembling lips. He said, "Great." I'll be building a new supermarket in north Leavenworth in a few months, and he would like me to come with him. I was stunned, what a low blow! Seems Art and Howard were going to build a second supermarket in the north part of Leavenworth and Howard would move to the new store, and Art would remain at the "old" store. The constant bickering would come to an end, and my job at Jahn's Supermarket would also come to an end when school was out in the spring of 1948. John and I would once again work on the farm in Kickapoo and I would be going to Army Reserve summer camp for two weeks at Fort Riley, Kansas. I hated to quit my job at the supermarket, but knew I wouldn't have time for a full-time job with all the other activities.

1928 Whippet
Bill and John's
first car

One Saturday during the spring of 1948 Pop had met a farmer from Missouri at the local sale barn who had a 1928 Whippet for sale. Pop knew John and I had been looking for a car and asked us if we wanted to buy the car. He told us the farmer wanted $75 for it and that it ran good, so John and I said, "Yes." We had most of the money saved up, and Pop loaned us the difference. The farmer drove the "Whippet" to Leavenworth the following Saturday; John and I became owners of our first car. It was a black, two-door sedan with wood-spoked wheels. It had a four-cylinder Willy-Overland engine. Willy-Overland later became Jeep, the work horse of the military during the 2nd World War and is still popular to this day, although it has undergone many changes. We were told by the farmer who sold it to us that when he bought "the Whippet" new, the big sales pitch was that the Whippet could accelerate to 60 miles per hour within a city block. We never proved the "pitch" to be correct as we had a hard time driving a full city block without a breakdown. We spent all our spare time working on the Whippet and learned a lot about the workings or non-workings of a "fine" automobile. I'm sure we pushed it for many more miles than the four-cylinder engine did. But we had a lot of fun with our first car.

Later that summer I spent two weeks at Fort Riley, Kansas, with the Army Reserve. We spent a lot of time learning about the weaponry of the Army and were involved with firing many of the weapons. We were also treated to a "mock" battle where we were spectators, sitting on a hillside and observing the mock battle below us in the valley.

After returning from summer camp, John and I worked on the farm for the remainder of the summer.

That fall I learned of a job opening at the local A&P (Atlantic & Pacific Tea Co.) grocery store, which was located between 5th and 6th Streets on Delaware. Kenneth Powell had worked all summer at the A&P behind the meat counter. Kenneth's brother, Bill, worked in the grocery department and told Kenneth about the vacancy. I applied for the job and, with my prior experience at Jahn's, was hired. The manager, Kenneth Hastings, was a good man to work for. He treated me as a valued employee, and I really enjoyed the time I worked at A&P. It was an old store which had been in the same location for many years, and this is where Mom and Pop had shopped during the depression. Mom's coffee of choice was the red bag of 8 O'Clock sold by the A&P.

Down the street a short distance, and in the same block, was Kroger's grocery store. Mom and Pop shopped both stores, depending on who had the best price on a given item, and up on 5th and Shawnee, about one and a half blocks away was the Big Jumbo grocery store, which was another store where Mom shopped.

Just east of the A&P Market was the J.C. Penney's store, which was also an old building with wooden floors. It had a balcony toward the rear of the store with merchandise, and also the office and cashier. As a young boy, I was always fascinated at the way you paid for your purchases and received your change. Clerks had several stations on the main floor where they would write up your order and then take your money and, along with the written order form, would place both in a small metal box. The box was then snapped onto a continuous belt that carried the box to the main cashier on the second floor. The cashier would make change and mark your receipt "paid," then send the little box back by way of the continuous belt. There were several belts which were always running.

During the war a person would shop where they could find a rationed item or with who had the best price. Downtown Leavenworth was a busy place, as most of the stores were concentrated in that area. Saturday, both day and night, was the shopping time of choice for most people in the area. Leavenworth was the shopping center for a very large area at that time, as the next large area with abundant stores was Kansas City, Kansas, and Kansas City, Missouri.

I worked after school and all day Saturday. Stocking shelves was the main job through the week, and boxing groceries and carrying them to cars was an all-day job on Saturday. All boxes that were emptied from stocking shelves were saved and stored by the checkout stands. Most customers preferred boxes to bags for their groceries. Thus, we were called "box boys." Now the same workers are called "baggers" or "sackers." After the store would close for the day, several of us would grab a broom and begin sweeping the old wood floor, after throwing out handfuls of treated sawdust on the floor to keep the dust down.

At that time the price was stamped on each item with an ink stamp. If there was a price change, it would be listed on a daily price change list and given out to all stockers. We would then change the price on can goods by using steel wool, rubbing out the old price and stamping the new price on it. This process was very time-consuming.

One Saturday, when reporting to work, Kenny, the manager, asked me to work the cheese and coffee counter as the regular man was off sick. I had reached my goal in life! To grind coffee all day was something I had dreamed about. The aroma of grinding coffee beans to this day will mentally return me to those days I worked at the A&P.

I worked at A&P grocery store until I graduated from high school in the summer of 1949.

CHAPTER 7

The Wheat Harvest

After graduation and the conclusion of school in May, Richard Simms, John and I decided to go to western Kansas and northern Oklahoma to work in the wheat harvest. We had sold the old 1928 Whippet at the sale barn for $25, which was $50 less than we had paid for it, but we were glad to get rid of all the prob-

Richard and Bill
Wheat Harvest — 1949

lems. John and I bought a 1935 Chrysler which was a good "old" car. It got about 50 miles to a quart of oil, but otherwise was a much better car than the Whippet.

We took our meager savings, and with a "huge" chocolate cake which Richard's mother had baked for us and a silver dollar from Titter "for luck," we headed for Wichita. After the first 50 miles, we made an "oil" stop and ate the huge chocolate cake.

We drove to Salina, Kansas, on old 40 Highway (now I-70), then south to Wichita. We took Highway 54 and went west to Liberal, Kansas, crossing the Cimarron River and headed south into the Oklahoma Panhandle. We stopped in Hooker, Oklahoma, I think, and parked along the main street trying to decide what to do next, when a farmer came up to the car and asked if we were looking for work. We said we had come west to work in the wheat harvest. He told us the harvest was still a couple of weeks away because of the unusually cool weather. He told us he had some work for us on his farm putting up hay and wanted to know if we would be interested. We looked at each other and quickly decided since we were about busted we would accept his offer. We followed the farmer out to his farm, which was a few miles from town, and almost at once started work. The farmer had his hay cut and wind-rowed. Richard climbed on the bailer and, after a short briefing from the farmer as to how to tie the wires, etc., took off bailing with the farmer driving the tractor. John and I began loading the bales onto a flatbed hay truck. We would drive, stop and load bales. When the truck had been loaded, we all drove to the barn and began stacking the bales of hay, then back to the field.

We quit work about 6 p.m. The farmer paid us for the work done, $1 per hour, and we took off to town to find a place to sleep. We discovered a small motel which rented for about $5 per night. We shared the cost and flipped to see who would shower first. We found a country restaurant nearby and ate supper. The next morning, after a short-stack pancake breakfast, we headed back to our haying job.

It had rained during the night, and the farmer said it was too wet to bale hay, but wanted us to go throughout the hayfield and turn all the bales that had been left from the day before so as to allow the sun to dry them. We did this for the remainder of the day and earned our $1 per hour. We stayed at the same motel that night and ate the same thing at the same little country restaurant.

It rained again that night and, reporting to the farmer the next morning, we were given the same task of turning wet bales of hay. The bales were now facing up the same as when baled. That evening at quitting time the farmer told us that if it rained again that night he would not need us until after the rains stopped and the alfalfa field was dry. It did rain again that evening, and we heard on the car radio, with all the rain and cool weather, the wheat harvest was still a week or two away. We knew it would be hard to find any work as long as the weather continued bad, so we decided to head back to Leavenworth.

We returned to Leavenworth by the same route, and spent the silver dollar that Titter had given me "for luck," for gas and oil in Lawrence, Kansas. We returned home broke, a fitting end to our great wheat harvest adventure.

Not long after our return to Leavenworth, our reserve unit, of which John was now a member, left for summer camp. We spent two weeks at Camp McCoy, Wisconsin. The two weeks were spent firing the 105mm Howitzer. We took turns at every position, and by the end of summer camp we were fairly proficient at setting up and firing the 105 Howitzer.

The end of summer camp found John and me without work. France and Vernard had started selling fruit and vegetables on weekends. They were still working at Fort Leavenworth, France at the Command and General Staff College and Vernard at the Fort Leavenworth Fire Department. They had their weekends free, so they would drive to the Kansas City Market early Saturday mornings and load up the cars with fruits and vegetables that were good sellers, such as bananas, watermelons, cantaloupes, apples, peaches, strawberries, etc., and lettuce, celery, green onions and many other produce items. They had started this venture in late spring of 1949, and business became so good that it became necessary to build a small building in which to sell their produce, and they also purchased a truck to haul the produce from Kansas City, Missouri.

This business became so time-consuming that France and Vernard quit their jobs at Fort Leavenworth, and the small market became a full-time job. By the time we returned from summer camp, John and I were hired to help at the market. The name, "Drive In Market," became well known as a place where "fresh" produce could be bought at a reasonable price, and the business flourished. I worked at the Drive In Market until the 14th of September.

Sue, Richard and Steve Simms.
Circa 1946.

CHAPTER 8

The Coast Guard Calls

ABOUT THE 1ST OF SEPTEMBER, Kenneth Powell, Raymond Kohler and I decided to join the Navy. We had talked about it for some time, so it wasn't a spur of the moment decision. We drove to Kansas City, Missouri, and to the Post Office downtown where the Navy Recruiting Office was located. We took our test and passed, except for Kenneth, who had a ruptured ear drum, unbeknownst to him, and failed to pass the physical. We asked the recruiter how long it would be before we were called. He said about six months. We told him that was too long a wait, as we wanted to go **now.** He said, "Sorry," so we didn't sign the papers. We walked out of the Post Office, contemplating what we should do, when we saw a sidewalk sign for the Coast Guard. We decided to try the Coast Guard, and Kenneth said he was going to sign up for the Air Force. Ray and I went to the Coast Guard Recruiting office and took all the tests, passed, and as with the Navy, asked when we could expect to be called. The Recruiter said about two weeks. We signed the paperwork and headed back to Leavenworth, two future Coast Guardsmen and an Airman.

One week later the Coast Guard called me and Ray and told us to be ready the next morning, as we would be picked up and driven to Kansas City to finish the processing. Ray and I had less than a day to clear up any unfinished business. I gave my share of the car to John, threw a few things in a small bag, said our good-byes, and early the next morning we were picked up by the Coast Guard and whisked away to Kansas City. We spent the rest of that day being processed into the service. We spent the night in a Kansas City YMCA, and early the next morning were driven to Union Station and put on a train for Philadelphia, where we caught another train for Atlantic City, New Jersey; then by bus to the Coast Guard Receiving Station in Cape May, New Jersey. Cape May is at the southernmost tip of New Jersey. The furthest I had ever been from home was to Oklahoma on our "wheat harvest" fiasco and the two weeks at Camp McCoy, Wisconsin.

That first night on the trip to Philadelphia, as I lay on my upper berth, I thought of the great adventure that lay ahead and also where I had come from, and the things that had made up my life to that point. I was not apprehensive because I had a good knowledge of the military, ROTC and the Army Reserve, and living through a war had been an education in itself. I had parents who believed in me, and although they were not happy to see me leave home, they knew it was what I wanted, and Mom and Pop supported my decision. They had always supported their children; no matter how dumb some of the things we did might seem to them, we could always count on their support.

****

We arrived in Philadelphia early in the morning on

the second day and had a short wait for our train to Atlantic City. We arrived in Atlantic City before noon and were picked up by a Coast Guard bus for our trip to Cape May, New Jersey. There were several new recruits on the bus, and when we arrived at the Coast Guard station in Cape May, there were several more who had arrived the night before.

The rest of the first day was spent getting our new uniforms and other clothing. We marched to a large barracks where we were shown how to roll our new clothes and pack in our sea bags. We stripped down and packed all our "street clothing" into a box for shipment home.

The second day was spent taking tests. The tests were designed to determine what specialty schools we might qualify for. My test scores showed I qualified for Cooks and Bakers school, Hospital Corpsman school, Electronics Technician school and Radio Operators school. I was asked which school I wanted, and I chose Radio Operators school. We didn't learn which school we would be attending until just before completing boot training.

The next day we started our training in earnest. Up at 5:00 a.m., make our bed, wash up, get dressed and fall in for chow. I was one of 40 which made up "P" Company. There were several other companies, and just about every week or so a Company was finishing their boot training and were being assigned duty stations or being sent to some specialty school.

Boot training lasted 12 weeks and covered everything from close order drills, firing range to seamanship. Seamanship included rowing a life boat, semifore flags, knot tying and a host of other things. We learned new terms and words pertaining to ships. Windows were port holes; hallways were companion ways; ceilings were overheads; stairs were ladders; floors were decks, and on and on.

Bill —
home on leave from boot camp
1949

In November, with about four weeks remaining in boot camp, we were loaded on a bus one Sunday afternoon and driven to Wildwood, New Jersey, for an afternoon of "fun." If you have ever been to Wildwood in November, you know that just about everything is boarded up for the winter. It was cold and windy that Sunday afternoon, and with little to do we were anxious to get back on the bus and get back to the Base. This was the only time we left the Base during our 12 weeks of boot camp.

We finished our boot training about the third week of December and were given two weeks leave. Those who qualified for specialty schools were notified before we left, and I learned that I would be going to Radio Operators school in Groton, Connecticut, when my two weeks leave ended.

Following my leave at home for Christmas and New Year's, I boarded the train at Union Station in Kansas City, Missouri, and headed for Groton, Connecticut; Groton is just across the Thames River from New London. It was at the training school when I saw television for the first time. It was a small screen TV, which was in the day room in the building in which we lived and trained. About the only thing I remember watching was wrestling.

The Radio Operators school was a six-month school. We had the duty every other weekend, cleaning the classrooms, the latrines and other areas and standing fire watches. On weekends when we didn't have the duty, we were free to leave the training school. A few of the guys who lived on the East Coast had cars, and we would drive to Hartford or New York City and see a stage show. One weekend a friend of mine who lived in Philadelphia invited me home to spend the weekend.

It was a German American family by the name of Krohler. When we sat down for the evening meal, the father would open up a large bottle of beer for each person at the table. I never drank beer before that time and had a difficult time downing the huge bottle. I think I left most of it, but it was a nice family and I had a great time.

Radio school ended in June 1950, the same month the Korean War broke out. We graduated from Radio school with the rank of Radioman 3rd Class. We received our orders for our first duty station. Some went to the West Coast, others to Alaska, and some stayed on the East Coast. I was to go to Guam and board a Coast Guard Buoy Tender, the USCGC Planetree.

The things I remember most about Groton, Connecticut, were: (1) Seeing the Coast Guard training ship, Eagle, under full sail heading down the Thames River for the Coast Guard cadets annual training cruise. The Coast Guard Academy was just across the river from Groton in New London. What a sight!! (2) Going to the Paramount Theatre in New York City and seeing a stage full of stars, all plugging their latest movies. In the group were Pat O'Brien, Kirk Douglas, Bob Hope and several others, and (3) driving to Hartford and seeing Xavier

Cougat and his orchestra with Gene Krupa at the drums. Upon leaving Groton, I boarded a train for Kansas City and two weeks leave at home.

At about this time on June 25, 1950, the Korean War started. The North Koreans fiercely raced into South Korea intent on destroying South Koreans and unifying both North and South Korea under Communist rule. Once again, we were involved in war.

When my leave ended, I was driven by John, Mom, Pop and Babe to Union Station in Kansas City for the long journey to Alameda Navy Base. I spent several days at Alameda waiting for transportation to Honolulu. The days were spent, along with several others, cutting grass and doing odd jobs. Finally we were loaded on board a huge Navy ship, a overhaul repair ship, for transport to Pearl Harbor. It took about five days to reach our destination, and the five days were spent standing radio watches, along with the regular crew members. The first day out the latrines were full of recruits, sailors heaving up their "guts." The seas were not that rough, but there were some very sick sailors. I wasn't affected by the sea and felt good until I went to the latrine. I didn't spend much time there.

I was standing on deck early on the fifth day and saw the Hawaiian Islands rise from the sea as we approached. It was a sight you never forget! Upon arriving at Pearl Harbor, I was picked up by the Coast Guard and taken to the Coast Guard base on Sand Island.

I was on Sand Island about a week waiting for transportation to Guam. While there, along with several others waiting for transportation, we did odd jobs, just anything to keep us busy.

It had been some time since I had been paid, as my records had not kept pace with me, and I was broke. So

I just stayed around the base. We were paid every two weeks in cash by the paymaster, but I had missed pay days because of all the travel.

One evening I was told to pack up and be ready to leave early the next morning. We were up early the next morning, got ready, ate and loaded up on trucks for a ride to Hickam Air Base. We loaded onto a four-engine B-26 Bomber, which had been converted somewhat in order to carry passengers. There were little jump seats along each side of the plane, and the bomb racks had been removed, which allowed for more seats down the center. To the best of my recollection, there were about 30 of us as passengers. We took turns going back and sitting in the tail gunner's seat. There wasn't anything to see, but for a short time we had a little area all our own. It was raining for part of our first day's flight, and it was restful watching the little rivulets of rain running down the plexiglas tail.

Late in the evening, just about dark, we landed on Wake Island and spent the night in a quonset hut. We were up early the next morning, and after eating breakfast in the chow hall, we loaded up for our final leg of the journey. It had been a long time since I had left radio school, and I was getting anxious to get to the ship and have a place I could call "home."

We landed late afternoon on Guam, and I was picked up by the Coast Guard and taken to the base on the north end of the Island. I spent the night there and was driven to the USCGC Planetree the next morning.

There were about 48 members in the crew, counting officers. The Captain was a tall, lean Lieutenant by the name of Richards from Newton, Kansas. During war time the Coast Guard is part of the Navy. During the 2nd World War, Lt. Richards was a Pacific fleet naviga-

USCGC Planetree Class Buoy Tender

tor, and after the war he reverted back to the Coast Guard.

The Planetree was a buoy tender and worked the islands north of Guam. A buoy tender, as the name implies, takes care of all the navigational aids in and around the harbors of several of the Pacific Islands. We also supplied material to several LORAN Stations. LORAN is Long Range navigation and sends out radio signals as an aid to ships and aircraft for navigational purposes.

After about a week on the Planetree and getting familiar with the radio room, we left Guam for a trip north to Okinawa. We stopped at several islands on the way: Saipan, Tinian and Pagan. The Planetree was a working ship, repairing buoys and setting new ones. There were three radiomen on the Planetree, and we stood radio watches 24 hours a day, four on and eight off around the clock. I had the 4 to 8 watch, 4:00 a.m. to 8:00 a.m. and 4:00 p.m. to 8:00 p.m.

There was a second buoy tender stationed at Guam.

The Ironwood made trips south to the Philippines and all islands in between. Ray Kohler, a friend who joined the Coast Guard at the same time as I did, was stationed aboard the Ironwood and worked in the engine room. We didn't get to see each other very much, as one or both of our ships were at sea most of the time.

Our trip to Okinawa took about two months, what with all the stops in between. We stayed in port about a month, and while in port the radiomen stood gangway watches, all but the radioman in charge. He did the daily duties, receiving weather and any messages for the Planetree.

We had the duty every other day. There wasn't much to do on Guam on our day off, but we did play a lot of baseball. We would take a team to the Coast Guard base and play their team. We had a movie on the fan tail a couple nights a week, but I missed most of them because of my watch hours.

I would get mail from home fairly often when we were in port, and it was about this time when Mom wrote and also sent a newspaper clipping about my old Army Reserve Unit, "B" Battery of the 758th Field Artillery Battalion, being called to active duty. John and France were now active members of the U.S. Army. John was sent to Fort Chaffee, Arkansas, for leadership training and then to Korea in 1951 with the 25th Infantry, 14th Infantry Regiment. France served as Captain of the Kansas Army Reserve Field Artillery Battery during the Korean War, 1951 to 1952.

Jim was recalled into the Army and spent his time at an Army hospital in Madison, Wisconsin; Bud was also recalled and stationed at a Naval hospital on the East Coast.

About a week prior to departure, the ship was re-

Leavenworth Reserve Unit on Active Duty

'B' BATTERY of the 758th Field Artillery Battalion, called to active duty, stood its first retreat yesterday afternoon in the Normandy Area at Fort Leavenworth. Front rank, left to right: M-Sgt. Leon Armour, M-Sgt. Anthony Gnip, M-Sgt. Paul Winstead, SFC John Cook, SFC Everett Drews, SFC John Junk, SFC Donald Kirkpatrick, SFC Leo Matzeler; second rank: Sgt. John Bergman, Sgt. Benjamin Douglas, Sgt. Gerald Hirschler, Sgt. Charles Keeton, St. Robert Lamborn, Sgt. Alvin Moll, Sgt. Paul W. Osthoff, Sgt. Willis Talbot; third rank: Sgt. George E. Williams, Sgt. Raymond Zoellner, Cpl. Loren Beaman, Cpl. Leroy Chinn, Cpl. Grover Dix, Cpl. Joe Elliott, Cpl. Louis Finneran,Cpl. Francis Stewart; fourth rank: Cpl. Ernest Taylor, Cpl. Raymond Tuttle, Cpl. Plummer Walker, Cpl. John Williams, Pfc. Joseph Corriston, Pfc. Howard Dix, Pfc. Donald Drews and Pvt. Donald Slifer. In the last rank the officers: Capt. Francis Williams, battery commander, 1st Lt. Hiram Mussett, 2nd Lt. Thomas Edmonds and 1st Lt. Frank Wilson. One man not in the picture is Cpl. Wayne Shipment, on the advance party.

supplied with the buoys that had been sandblasted or repainted, along with large concrete sinkers that were used to anchor the buoys in place. All material for another long trip was loaded aboard. Several hundred 55-gallon drums of fuel oil were loaded aboard. The hold was full of buoys, sinkers and chains, so the fuel drums were lashed down on the fan tail. This would prove to almost undo the Planetree. The fuel oil would go to the LORAN station on Iwo Jima. We departed Guam early one morning and headed north to Iwo Jima.

The first few days went smooth and routine. We started receiving weather reports that the weather was building and reaching gale strength. The next day we began to run into heavy seas, and through the day the seas and wind became very heavy, and we were right in the middle of the gale.

The old Planetree was rolling, and with the weight of the fuel drums above the water line she was slow in recovering, and it wouldn't get any better for the next three days. The Captain made a run for a small island west of us. We reached it on the third day and anchored on the lee side and rode out the storm.

The storm passed and we resumed our trip to Iwo Jima. A few days later we arrived and anchored off shore. The LORAN station sent out a duck, and we began unloading the supplies.

From Iwo Jima, we headed for Chi Chi Shima. Chi Chi Shima is the island where former President George Bush's plane was shot down by the Japanese during WWII. He survived and was picked up by a submarine.

We anchored off shore since there were no docks where our ship could moor. We took the whale boat ashore and spent the day looking at the fortification that the Japanese had built for the defense of the island. The mountains surrounded a bay, and the mountains had been hollowed out for gun implacements and living quarters for the defenders. The island was so well

Chi Chi Shima residents out for ship's meal

fortified that the U.S. simply bypassed the island on the way to Tokyo.

That evening a boatload of the inhabitants came out to the ship for a meal aboard the Planetree. After they departed the ship, we pulled anchor and headed for Okinawa. The stop at Chi Chi Shima had been a goodwill stop.

We spent Christmas 1951 in Okinawa. The storm we had ridden out had cut our food supply aboard ship to almost zero, and we ate a lot of beans the last few days before arriving at Okinawa where we were re-supplied.

One day on the intercom we heard, "Fire crew report to the buoy deck; this is not a drill." Since I was a member of the "fire crew," I reported. We were all loaded on a truck and headed inland a short distance to a small inlet from the sea. The whole inlet was on fire. Seems a huge pipe line carrying aviation fuel from the dock area to the Air Force base, which set up on higher ground and quite a distance from the dock, had ruptured at a point where it crossed over the inlet. There was a small village surrounding one side of the inlet, and the houses were in danger of burning.

128

The Air Force was fighting the fire with a couple of tanker fire trucks from the air base, which was several miles away. They were laying down foam on the water trying to smother the flames, but about the time this was accomplished, the truck would run out of water and have to return to base for refill. The other truck would arrive and the same thing would happen.

There was a stiff breeze blowing, which would blow the foam away, allowing the fuel to re-ignite. We had brought with us a gasoline-powered pump called a "Handy Billy." The suction end hose was placed in the inlet, and our fire hose was placed on the discharge end, giving us a stream of water much more powerful than the pumper trucks. Our nozzle man was a big man from Texas. I was second man, holding the five-gallon bucket of foam material. There was a tube directly behind the nozzle which was used to suction the foam material from the bucket and mix it with the stream of water. There was a man directly behind me who was holding and pulling the fire hose. Others were carrying foam buckets out to us. We started out across the inlet, which was about waist deep, spraying foam.

The Air Force stopped at this point and was helping pass their foam to us. It took a while, but we managed to completely cover the inlet with foam and, though we had successfully put out the fire, a gust of wind blew the foam away from around us, and the fuel re-ignited.

The pipe line valve had been closed at the source, but there was a large quantity of fuel in the line. The man on the nozzle swung the nozzle around in circles, and we finally had the inlet covered again. After a short period of time, the surface had cooled and the fire was out.

We were covered from the top of our heads down with sticky, gooey foam. It had been a long two or three

Bill — Radio Room
USCGC Planetree, 1950

hours, and we were glad to get back to the ship and clean up.

Before we left Okinawa shortly after Christmas, we received a letter of commendation from the Commanding Officer of the U.S. Air Force base. They also wanted information on our "Handy Billy." They are a common piece of equipment with fire departments today, but they were a fairly new item back then.

****

We arrived back at Guam to learn that the Ironwood had been ordered back to Pearl Harbor for dry dock. They were also to have some 20mm guns mounted on their flying bridge. The Korean war had started on June 25, 1950, and I guess the Government wasn't too keen on having ships in the North Pacific that were unarmed. We also learned that we would be making the run south to the Philippines. We were in port only long enough to re-supply, then headed south.

There were 12 Coast Guard LORAN stations in the Pacific. We took care of six on our northern run, and now we would re-supply the six on this southern run.

Our first stop was Ulithi, then Mog Mog, where we anchored off shore and were allowed to go ashore and look around. Mog Mog was a very primitive island. The natives lived in grass huts. The stop was more of a good will visit. We stayed only a few hours, then on to the

Philippines where we tied up at Subic Bay. We stayed in Manila for a couple of days, then headed for the LORAN station on Borneo, where we anchored off shore and the LORAN station sent a duck out to pick up supplies, and took a bunch of us ashore to see their base. The LORAN station was next to a native village, and it was strange seeing the natives walking around the Coast Guard base. After the supplies had been off-loaded from the ship, we returned to the ship and departed for our return trip to Guam. We worked some buoys on the way back.

Upon arriving in Guam, we learned we would be going back to Pearl Harbor for dry dock and would be fitted with some 20mm guns. The Ironwood was due back in a few days and would cover our area while we were gone.

On its way back to Pearl Harbor, we would make one stop at Eniwetok and pull and replace one large channel buoy. During the trip to Eniwetok the deck crew worked on a huge buoy to be placed in the entrance to Eniwetok. The huge buoy was a lighted bell buoy. All new batteries, nine large batteries in all, are placed in three compartments in the buoy. The buoy was sandblasted and painted and was ready to be set.

We arrived at Eniwetok and found out that we would have to be finished by about 9:00 p.m. and depart the island as an atom bomb was to be tested at 6:00 a.m. the next day, and since we were not equipped with the necessary safety gear, we would have to be a certain distance from the blast site.

Everything was going as planned, the old buoy was pulled and the new buoy was prepared to be set. In setting a large buoy, the buoy is positioned on the edge of the buoy deck, which is just about four or five feet from the water. The large sinker or anchor is positioned and balanced on the edge of the deck also. The anchor chain is attached to the sinker and the other end to the base of the buoy. The anchor chain is flaked out on the deck and is just long enough so that when the sinker hits the bottom, the buoy will float and not move more than a few feet from the correct position. The seaman cut the line that was holding the sinker with an ax. The sinker went over the side taking the chain with it. The last thing to go is the buoy. The buoy went as planned. It floated for a few seconds, then began to sink. We could see the light flashing as it sank out of sight. Seems the sinker had hit the proper ledge, but slipped off.

Another buoy was prepared, the one we had just lifted. It was quickly sand-blasted, painted, and new batteries installed. We were working against the clock now. We had to be out by 9:00 p.m. and it was now about 6:00 p.m. A new sinker was positioned, new anchor chain installed, and this all took time, because we are talking some heavy material.

Everything went well though, and the new buoy was launched and stayed where it was supposed to. We got out of there a little after 9:00 p.m. I had the 4:00 a.m. to 8:00 a.m. radio watch the next day and stepped out on deck at 6:00 a.m. to see if I could see the A-Bomb blast, but the sun was up by then and it was too light to see the blast.

It took 30 days to travel from Guam to Pearl Harbor. The Planetree would only do about nine knots, so it was literally "a slow boat from China." Upon our arrival in Pearl Harbor, several of the personnel were transferred off the ship for duty elsewhere. Myself and one other radioman were transferred to the Radio Station on Oahu. The radio station was located on a high area overlooking the ocean at Wailupi. It was a very pretty area, and the radio station was kept in immaculate condition. Huge coconut palms were everywhere. I really enjoyed my stay at the radio station. After six months I was transferred back to the States.

My next duty station was the Radio Station in Long Beach, California. The radio station and light house were located at Point Vincente in Palos Verdes Estates. We were high above the Pacific and could see whales at certain times of the year. I also enjoyed my stay in Long Beach.

I had been at the radio station about six months when I noticed on the bulletin board one day that the Coast Guard was about to put several ships in commission. The Navy had given the Coast Guard some WWII destroyer escorts that were in moth balls in Green Cove Springs, Florida. The bulletin said that anyone interested in transferring to one of the ships should put in their request. Radiomen were needed, so I applied and a short time later found out I had been accepted.

It took several weeks to get the ships cleaned up from all the goo which had been sprayed on them. Green Cove Springs is located on the Saint John's River, just south of Jacksonville. The river was fresh water, and that's why it was chosen: less rust.

After a month or so we were ready to travel, and the USCGC Richey headed up the East Coast to the Philadelphia Naval Shipyards for dry dock. We were in dry dock for about a month, and during that time the crew attended several Navy schools, including Fire Fighters' school. After dry dock, we went to Baltimore Shipyards to have a weather shack added to the fantail.

From Baltimore, we sailed to Norfolk, Virginia, to be fueled and pick up our ammunition, including depth charges. We then went out for sea trials which lasted several days. We put back into Norfolk, and then found out that the Richey would be going through the Panama Canal and on to Midway as our home port. A few days prior to sailing, an order came down that anyone on the ship with six months or less on their enlistment would be transferred off the ship and sent to a duty station close to their home. My orders came through — I would be going to the Coast Guard radio station in St. Louis, Missouri.

Ray Kohler, whom I had enlisted with, was stationed on a cutter which worked the Mississippi and Missouri Rivers and whose base was St. Louis. We had a chance to visit several times and drive home to Leavenworth a couple of times a month.

My discharge date was coming up, and I had decided to leave the Coast Guard when we got the word that everyone was going to have their service time extended by six months, what a blow! The Korean War was winding down, and two months into my six months extension, the Government said we could be discharged. So in November I was discharged and headed home. Ray Kohler decided to reenlist for three more years.

So ended my Coast Guard career!

CHAPTER 9

Return to Civilian Life

WHEN I RETURNED to Leavenworth, I started working for France at the Drive-In Market, which had grown into a fairly large business. Vernard had opened a liquor store in one corner of the Market, which was a separate business from the Market.

Later in November, John returned home from Korea wearing the Combat Infantry Badge, Service Medal with one bronze campaign star, and the United Nations Service Medal, John told me that while in Korea his squad nicknamed him "Snake." They all said they had never seen anyone get as low to the ground as John when the North Koreans began shooting at them.

Shortly after returning home, John began working at the Drive-In Market. It was a good job, but hard work. At one time, the whole family except for Pop, Mom and Titter worked at the Market. Jim would work there on his days off from his prison job, and Bud, who had since transferred from Leavenworth, would work at the Market when they were home on vacation. Titter was now married to Mike Dardis, and they were living in North Dakota. Babe worked in the Market as a checker until she moved to Topeka, where she later married

Drive-In Market
Jerry Dykes, France and Freda

John in Korea

John in Korea
1951

Margie, Titter,
Babe, Mary
and Kathy
"8 Mile" House
1955

and moved to California.

Pop and Mom had sold the farm in Kickapoo and purchased an 80-acre farm north of Leavenworth. The farm was known as the "8 Mile" house; a large two-story rock house with quite a history. When I arrived home from the service, Pop and Mom were in the process of buying the 8 Mile farm, and

Helen and John
Circa 1976

we would move not long after I got home.

On February 7, 1953, John married his high school sweetheart, Helen Hiatt.

In the summer of 1953 I decided to go to Air Traffic Control school in Kansas City. I had the G.I. Bill and didn't want to spend the rest of my life trimming lettuce and cauliflower. I went to Kansas City on my day off and registered for school, which was to start in September. I had made the decision.

The next day at work I was about to tell John what I had done, but before I could tell him, he said he had gone to Kansas City the day before and registered for classes at the University of Missouri, Kansas City. I thought both of us could not leave France at the same time, so I cancelled my registration at Air Traffic Control school in K.C. I guess I felt at that time I would be trimming lettuce and cauliflower for the rest of my life!

In 1954 John asked me to go with him to the office where Helen was working (the County Attorney's office), as Helen wanted him to bring a book to her; I went along with him. The office was on the second floor of the Axa Building, over Mehl & Schott's Drug store. Next door to the County Attorney's office of Col. Boone was the City Attorney's office

*Margie and Bill, Wedding Day
June 14, 1955*

of Tom Brown. His secretary was Marjorie Behee, and she was in Helen's office at the time I was there. I met her for the first time. I liked what I saw and later called and asked Margie for a date, and she accepted. On our first date we doubled with John and Helen for dinner and an evening at Randle's, outside Atchison, Kansas. Our second date was to see the Ice Capades in Kansas City.

Margie and I hit it off from the beginning, and I was well accepted by her family, except for the time I got Margie home after midnight and the door was locked and we had to ring the doorbell. Margie's mother, Dorothy, came to the door and let Margie in. She didn't say anything to me, but I could tell by her look that this kind of behavior would not be tolerated.

On June 14, 1955, Margie and I were married; it was a Tuesday, as this was the day the Drive-In Market closed for a day for our wedding. I did get a week off for our honeymoon; we traveled to beautiful Colorado Springs, Colorado.

* * * * *

It was in March or April 1956 that France called me aside one day and told me that he and Freda were going to sell the Market and buy a resort on the Lake of the Ozarks. He told me

Proud Dad and Bob, 7 weeks

that if I could find a job to take it. I found one and took it. The job was assistant manager for a finance company in Leavenworth. It was all new to me, but I enjoyed the work.

On May 3, 1956, Margie gave birth to our son, Robert Thomas. He weighed almost 9 lbs. and 22" long, had dark eyes and lots of dark hair — a real prize!! He was our pride and joy and the envy of everyone in the nursery!

In the fall of 1956, France called one day to say that the resort deal had fallen through and wanted to know if I would come back to work for him. I told him I liked my job and had gotten a couple of raises. France said he would match it, so I told him I would come back to work for him. I gave my two weeks notice to the finance company. The home office for the company was in Topeka, and the "big wheel" from the home office came to Leavenworth and tried to convince me to stay, but I had made my decision, along with Margie's approval. So it was back to lettuce and cauliflower.

In the spring of 1957 France had the opportunity to purchase the American Motors dealership in Leavenworth. The

Bob, 3-1/2 years 1959

Drive-In Market was closed and all the equipment sold, and Vernard expanded the liquor store to include all the area formerly occupied by the Market. I went to work for France as parts manager in the AMC dealership. It sure beat trimming cauliflower!

Bud and Jim had talked with me about taking the test for the Federal Prison Service, so in the summer of 1959 I decided to take the test at the local post office — and passed. In April of 1960, I, along with 15 others, was called to report for training at the U.S. Prison, Leavenworth, Kansas. Thus a new chapter in my life, and also my family's life, began because after two months training at the USP Leavenworth, all but two of the new class were transferred to the newly opened Federal Correctional Institution in Lompoc, California.

****

I could continue on with the 20-plus years I worked in the Federal Prison system, but I'll save that for another book some day. But I think I will bring this to an end because I believe I have done what I set out to do. I wanted to show how a family of ten came through a depression and two wars intact and cared for each other through thick and thin.

On looking back on my life, I mostly remember the good times and tend to disregard the unpleasant things; they tend to only cloud the issue.

I list the good things in order of their importance. God would most certainly come first, for if not for him I would never have met and married my wonderful and caring wife, Margie, and if not for God, we would not have had such a great son, Bob, and daughter-in-law, Cindy, and three great grandchildren, Tim, Karie and Melissa. And also I would never have been born into such a **grand family** and given an opportunity to have such great memories.

* * * * * * * * * *

THE TRUE JOY OF LIFE IS THE JOURNEY

Sometimes in the afternoons, Mom would have a few minutes free time from all her many household duties. She loved to read and would enjoy a good detective story. Sometimes she would try her hand at poetry. The following page reflects one of her best, entitled AUTUMN.

* * * * * * * * * *

Thanks to Babe and her daughter, Carolyn, who had this poem preserved and sent it for my birthday several years ago.
I treasure it!

Autumn

When beauty walks the autumn hills,

and paints the leaves with gold,

I lift my eyes up to the trees

its wonders to behold,

And see the masters touch on high,

where ever my eyes may stray,

and I bow my head in humble thanks,

for this beautiful Autumn day............

Beulah E. Williams

OUR FAMILY

Williams Family Updates

Pop and Mom sold the "8 mile house" farm, and retired to a home in Leavenworth. Pop continued to work part-time selling cars for France at the AMC dealership. Pop died in 1963 and Mom in 1970.

Bud continued to work for the Bureau of Prisons, and was associate warden at the Federal Prison in Lewisburg, PA. at the time of his death in 1971. Bud's wife, Ruth, lives with their oldest daughter, Judy, in Georgia. Their other daughters are Bobbie, Linda and Nancy.

France sold the American Motors dealership in 1972 and retired. He and his wife, Freda, loved to travel. He died in 1982. Freda died in 1988. Their daughter, Ann, is married and has two children, Chris and Amy, and lives in the San Diego area.

Sis died in 1973 at the age of 52 from complications following surgery. Her husband, Vernard, died in 1984. They had a son, Gerald, an attorney in Kansas. He and his wife, Pam, have two children.

Jim retired from the Prison Service in 1974 as the hospital administrator at the U.S. Penitentiary in Safford, Arizona. They were living in El Paso, Texas, at the time of his death in 1976. His wife, Marguherita, moved to Leavenworth, and died in 1990. They had two children, David and Valerie.

Titter retired a few years ago and lives in Eudora, Kansas. Her second oldest daughter, Kathy, died in 1981. Her husband, Mike, died in 1998. Titter loves to travel and spends time with each of their children: Mary Shuman, Patrick, Mark, Gregory, Jeffrey, Michael "Mickey," Anne Perry and John, who lives at home.

John died in 1987, while still working as training supervisor for New York Life Insurance Co. office in Topeka,

Kansas. His wife, Helen, and son, Stephen, live in Topeka.

Babe lives in Redlands, CA. and teaches Special Aids classes, having earned her degree in Education. Her husband is deceased. Babe loves to travel, spending time with her five children, Terri, Carolyn, Paul, Evan and Walter.

March 2001

Final Thoughts

This book has given me the opportunity to look back on the 70 years of my life. I would not have changed a thing. Oh, maybe some minor things, as hindsight is always better. But if I had it all to do over, I would not change a thing. I would still want to have been born on May 23, 1930, during a depression when times were hard and when we really appreciated the simple things of life. A good, hot meal on a cold winter evening, sitting around the supper table, an oil lamp, with parents, brothers and sisters who could laugh at the hard times, and knew deep down that things would be better.

It took many years, but things did get better. It's hard for me to look at today's youth and picture them coming through that period with the same positive outlook. But then I look at my grandchildren, my nieces and nephews and see that look in their eyes, that same look I saw in my parents, brothers and sisters. They could do it, but I hope they never have to.